Patton's Eyes in the Sky

USAAF Combat Reconnaissance Missions
North-West Europe 1944-1945

Patton's Eyes in the Sky

USAAF Combat Reconnaissance Missions
North-West Europe 1944-1945

Tom Ivie

CLASSIC
An imprint of
Ian Allan Publishing

Tom Ivie has studied and written about Second World War aviation history for many years. His interest was inspired when he assembled research material and conducted interviews with the veterans who flew the accurate scale models of aircraft he built in his spare time.

As a result of his friendship with the late John H. Hoefker, an ace with the 10th Photo Reconnaissance Group, he was introduced to many veterans of the 10th PRG and the idea for this book was born.

He is a graduate of Eastern Kentucky University and served as an officer in the US Army for six and a half years. He works as a buyer of developmental parts and equipment for a leading manufacturer of aircraft engines in the US Midwest.

Tom Ivie is the author of *Aerial Reconnaissance: The 10th Photo Recon Group in WWII* (1981), *Fighters of the Mighty Eighth* (with William N. Hess) (1990), *The Blue Nosed Bastards of Bodney: The 352nd Fighter Group in WWII* (with Robert H. Powell Jr.) (1990), *Mustang Aces* (with William N. Hess) (1992) and *The 352nd Fighter Group* (2002). He has also written numerous articles for *Air Classics* magazine and for the journal of the Friends of the USAF Museum Foundation.

First published 2003

ISBN 1-903223-26-1

Produced by Chevron Publishing Limited
Project Editor: Robert Forsyth
Cover and book design by Colin Woodman Design

Published by Classic Publications

an imprint of Ian Allan Publishing Ltd, Hersham, Surrey KT12 4RG

Printed by Ian Allan Printing Ltd, Hersham, Surrey KT12 4RG

Visit the Classic Publications website at www.classic-books.co.uk

CONTENTS

INTRODUCTION

Throughout history man's inability to live with his neighbors, or a tyrant's greed for power has resulted in an endless succession of wars. The warring nations have each tried to build the most powerful, well-armed, and best-led armies. In all wars the average fighting man has done his duty admirably, and a few have demonstrated outstanding heroics and bravery. However, history has proved that it is not always the country that fields the most powerful army that comes out on top. The commander that develops a good intelligence system and uses his information correctly has often defeated more powerful forces. This information, or intelligence, as it is referred to in the military, is generally supplied by two distinct sources; espionage – in which spies work in the enemy's own territory – or combat intelligence gained through reconnaissance units.

In its early days reconnaissance was performed primarily by scouts, men who were very fleet of foot, who upon learning something about the enemy's intentions raced back to report it to their unit. As time went on the horse played a role in reconnaissance work, as evidenced by America's Indian Wars, when frontiersmen who knew the Indian's territory and habits were hired as scouts for the cavalry. Ground scouts or reconnaissance units still exist today and are quite effective as evidenced by their work in the Persian Gulf War of 1991 and the war against terrorism today. This book deals, however, with aerial reconnaissance, which probably represents one of the most significant changes in the history of combat intelligence.

Aerial reconnaissance was first used by the French Army as far back as 1794, when on 2 June, Colonel Jean-Marie Countelle, the commanding officer of the French "Air Force" made his initial ascent in a balloon at Maubeug. From his vantage point Colonel Countelle was able to observe the enemy's movements north-east of the city and his observations enabled French forces to win the battle. It was also the French who first began attempts at aerial photography. The earliest recorded attempts are experiments by Colonel Aime Lassudat, who attempted to make topographic maps for the French Corps of Engineers. Gaspard F. Tourchon was the first to recognize and demonstrate the military value of aerial photography. He had written to the General Staff about having a better "belfry" than the standard use of church steeples as observation posts, and proved his idea would work in 1858 when he photographed a village from an altitude of 250 feet.

It was during the American Civil War that the military put aerial reconnaissance to work for them. After two balloonists, John Allen and John Wise, failed in their attempts, another balloonist, John LaMountain succeeded. In August 1861 his captive balloon was operated from a ship anchored off Hampton Roads, Virginia and on his first aerial mission LaMountain observed heavy concentrations of Confederate artillery batteries positioned to fire on Fort Monroe. As a result of his work Union forces surprised the Rebels and captured their guns. He was also credited for providing a good estimate of enemy strength in the area by counting campfires that he observed from his balloon. In the fall of 1861 LaMountain made several free ascent flights over the Confederate lines, sketched their positions and brought back important information to the Union Army. His activities were finally halted in November 1861 when high winds broke his balloon away from its tether and it disappeared.

Probably the most successful balloonist during the American Civil War was Professor Thaddeus S. C. Lowe. During his service with the Union Army, Lowe made over 3,000 reconnaissance flights and vastly improved the art of aerial reconnaissance. During this period Lowe provided valuable information to the Union Army through his observations; developed aerial artillery adjustment by use of the telegraph; developed a signal system of phosphorescent balloons, and improved aerial photography by coming up with a photo enlarger that enabled the famous photographer, Matthew Brady, to enlarge aerial photos from three to 20 inches. In spite of his outstanding contribution to the war effort, Lowe was often misunderstood and misused by the military and as a result he resigned his post in 1863. By war's end, however, even his detractors had to admit that he had rendered a tremendous service to the United States Army and that he had set a pattern for things to come.

The US Army's last use of the aerial balloon for reconnaissance was during the Spanish-American War when Lt. Colonels Joseph Maxwell and George Derby went aloft in an effort to determine enemy defensive positions. From their observation post above the fighting on San Juan Hill, Maxwell and Derby noted a new route for General Shafter to send up replacements and adjust fire into the Spanish positions, thereby ensuring a decisive American victory.

The advent of the airplane has changed the world in many ways, and one of the most dramatic of the changes has been its use in wartime. In spite of the usual reluctance of the "Top Brass" to try any new and untested tactics, some forward-looking aviators began to look into the use of aircraft for observation purposes. The first true observation mission was flown by Lt. Benjamin Foulois during the 1911 Texas Maneuvers. Since the lieutenant did not spot the "enemy" the US Army considered his experiment a failure, but the determined young officer did not give up. The following year he was ordered to take part in the Connecticut Maneuvers and this time was able to provide excellent intelligence to the forces he was supporting. In 1916, after Pancho Villa raided New Mexico, President Woodrow Wilson ordered General John J. Pershing into Mexico to track him down. When General Pershing deployed his troops into Mexico he included the 1st Aero Squadron, and for the first time, the US Air Service was used in a foreign land. The significance of the Mexican expedition to aerial reconnaissance was that it was able to observe and photograph areas in which the infantry and cavalry could not effectively operate. This proved to the many skeptics that the airplane could be a very important addition to the nation's military strength and resulted in a high appropriation from Congress for aviation research.

By the time the United States entered the First World War, both the Germans and the Allied forces had had nearly three years to develop observation and photo reconnaissance tactics. It is not known who made the first successful use of photo reconnaissance in the war, but once its worth was discovered, both sides began widespread use of it.

Throughout the years, military aviators have been painted as gallant, romantic figures by writers and Hollywood alike. The chief character has been the dashing fighter pilot, and secondly the hard working bomber-pilot. Both the fighter- and the bomber pilot did an outstanding and heroic job and deserve much credit for their work. On the other hand, there has been little said or written about the less glamorous job of the reconnaissance pilots and crews, whose mission was to fly a certain route or line and report the activities of the enemy. Why? It is just routine many believe, but if they gave it some thought they would realize that the reconnaissance pilot had one of the most difficult, most dangerous, and in many cases, the least appreciated job of all military pilots.

The static trench warfare of the First World War highlighted both the importance and dangers of aerial reconnaissance missions. Because of the trench warfare strategy practiced by both sides, artillery duels became a common occurrence and as a result, aerial observation and photographing of the opposition's positions and movements were of paramount importance. In those days the camera was still a quite primitive instrument and required a stable, slow-flying aircraft flown by an excellent pilot and crewed by a skilled cameraman in order to accomplish the mission. The importance of these vital missions made these aircraft the target of every gun the enemy could bring to bear, both on the ground and in the air. Many a famous fighter pilot of that era built his reputation on the destruction of the enemy's observation aircraft and balloons. Probably the two best examples are Germany's Manfred von Richthofen and Lt. Frank Luke of the United States Air Service. The Red Baron of Germany listed 45 observation aircraft among his 80 kills, and Frank Luke, in an intensive 45 days, destroyed four aircraft and 14 observation balloons before he was killed while trying to destroy another balloon. Both men received the highest decoration for valor bestowed by their respective nations for their exploits. As aerial tactics developed the fighter pilot was given two important tasks, i.e. protecting his own observation planes and destroying the enemy's. In spite of the perpetual danger these pioneers of photo reconnaissance stuck doggedly to their tasks and during the course of the First World War, American observation took 18,000 photos that were developed into 585,000 prints and distributed to all levels of command. The courage shown by these men proved worthwhile because they developed a technique that is still used to ensure the existence of nations. The Cuban missile crisis of 1962 is an excellent example of how a

A Salmson 2 A2 flown by the 12th Aero Squadron in the First World War. The squadron was assigned to the 1st Observation Group in April 1918 and saw continuous action from June 1918 until the end of the war on 11 November 1918. (credit: Air Force Museum)

The Fairchild F-1A (later C-8A) was the US Army's first aircraft built especially for the purposes of photo reconnaissance. (*credit: Air Force Museum*)

nuclear war was possibly averted through the use of aerial photo reconnaissance and photo interpretation.

At least two of the squadrons that later became part of the 10th Photo Reconnaissance Group were activated during the First World War. The 12th Aero (Observation) Squadron saw combat duty in France from December 1917 to 11 November 1918, and then became a part of the Army of Occupation. The 15th Aero Squadron was based in New York. From January 1918 until the end of the war, it provided aerial reconnaissance along the north Atlantic seaboard.

At the end of the First World War interest in military aviation typically took a plunge and appropriations and progress both suffered. The wartime vision of observation squadrons still prevailed; consequently the operational aircraft and the new ones designed for reconnaissance purposes were still slow and vulnerable. On the other hand, some important steps in the development of aerial cameras were being made. In 1919 Dr. George Goddard was appointed to the position of officer-in-charge of aerial photographic research at McCook Field, Dayton, Ohio. Under Dr. Goddard's guidance several revolutionary new concepts were developed to include: infrared photography and long-range photography; plans for aircraft especially designed for photo reconnaissance; special cameras for these aircraft, and one other very important item for combat units, the portable field laboratory unit. Probably one of the most significant developments made

Photographs taken with a Sonne Strip camera by the 34th PS during its training period in North Carolina. (*credit: Ben Rosen*)

The Curtis O-52 Owl was used by the 12th and 15th Observation Squadrons during the period 1940-42 but proved to be unpopular among members of these squadrons. (*credit: Air Force Museum*)

during Dr. Goddard's leadership was the long focal length cameras that were later put to excellent use in the Second World War. Another important development he played a part in was the photographic mapping of portions of the United States.

In 1926 the US Army Air Service became the US Army Air Corps and with the new status it gained by being a combat arm of the Army, new funds were allocated. An early task assigned the new USAAC was to photo-map the east and west coasts of Florida and the results were so exceptional that funding to photo-map an additional 35,000 square miles of territory was quickly provided. The additional funding allowed Dr. Goddard to experiment with the new Bagley K-3 triple-lens camera, and to develop waterproof paper, both of which would play a big part in aerial photography. Unfortunately the government's generosity did not carry over to aircraft development, and funding for new aircraft was so limited that it allowed for the design of only one new type of aircraft, the Fairchild F-1A. Six of these aircraft were ordered for the Army at a total cost of $137,192.35.

By 1931 some of the Army and Navy "Brass" were beginning to recognize the potential of aerial reconnaissance, and the historic agreement between General Douglas MacArthur and Admiral

This flight of five North American O-47As of the 15th Observation Squadron was photographed as it crossed the Ohio River during the maneuvers of 1940. (*credit: Robert Anderson*)

The Stinson O-49 was utilized briefly by several Observation Squadrons during the period 1939-42. (*credit: Air Force Museum*)

William Pratt was real progress, a key part of which was the division of defense responsibilities between the two Services. Under the agreement the Army would be responsible for defense of America's coastlines and its overseas possessions while the Navy would base its aircraft with the Fleet. In the years following the agreement the USAAC tested its long-range reconnaissance ideas in three important missions: the flight of B-10 bombers to Alaska in 1935, the 1937 interception of the battleship USS *Utah*, and the 1938 interception of the Italian liner *Rex*. These missions proved the worth of long-range reconnaissance, and in the case of the Alaska mission, valuable lessons were learned about extremely cold weather photography.

As war began to approach it became obvious that the United States would need people who were trained to take and interpret photos, and in 1939 such a course was developed. Following the German invasion of Poland in September 1939, the course was expanded dramatically, and a course to train aerial photographers to operate in bombers was initiated. Another step in the right direction was the development of the S-2 strip camera by Fred Sonne that could be used in high-speed/low-altitude photography. As it appeared increasingly likely that America would become involved sooner or later in the war, Captain Harvey C. Brown, Jr. was sent to Britain for a photography course. During his stay he met the photo interpreter Constance Babbington-Smith who amazed him with the information and facts she could glean from a photo. Dr. George Goddard was also in England at this time and was very impressed by the photo reconnaissance work performed by the Royal Air Force. Upon his return to the United States he reported his findings to the government and insisted that the country develop faster and better aircraft for photo reconnaissance purposes. Sadly, Washington did not listen to Captain Brown or Dr. Goddard, and it was not until the British warned the US government that the Japanese were flying over the Gilbert Islands and photographing them that Washington took notice. By the time a decision was made to photograph Japanese installations in the Pacific, it was too late. In fact one of the long-range aircraft scheduled to carry out a reconnaissance mission over some of these installations was parked in Hawaii on 7 December 1941. Consequently no real aerial reconnaissance was carried out and the apathy shown by America's leaders after the British warning resulted in the disgrace of Pearl Harbor.

While the principles of long-range reconnaissance were being developed during the mid and late 1930s, observation aircraft and tactics continued to dwell in the past. For the most part they continued to fly short-range missions in support of or in cooperation with the ground forces. The reconnaissance squadrons were attached to bomber groups and flew modified bombers, but this practice was to prove ineffective and costly during the early stages of the Second World War.

When America entered the Second World War its observation squadrons were still flying aircraft that were ponderous and obsolete for modern warfare. This outmoded thinking would have had excellent pilots risking their lives flying observation missions in aircraft such as the O-47, O-49 and O-52. The 10th Photo Reconnaissance Group and its predecessor, the 73rd Observation Group, were heavily involved in the transition from these outmoded concepts to the development of modern photo and tactical reconnaissance techniques, a role that played an important part in the defeat of Nazi Germany. This is their story.

ACKNOWLEDGEMENTS

The author received the generous assistance of many people in the preparation of this history of the 10th Photo Reconnaissance Group. Without it this project could not have been undertaken, and to them a great debt of gratitude is owed. The idea for this history was born out of the author's friendship with the late John H. Hoefker, who served with distinction with the 15th Tactical Reconnaissance Squadron, and was developed in 1974 when the 10th Photo Reconnaissance Group held its first reunion.

A lion's share of the credit for this project must go to the late Newton E. Jarrard, who provided needed assistance in many ways. He introduced the author to many individuals who served with the Group, purchased microfilm of the Group's records for use in this project, provided numerous photos and documents from his personal files, and led the way in assisting in the search for "lost" veterans of the 10th Photo Reconnaissance Group. In addition to his material help, his constant enthusiasm and encouragement went a long way in seeing this history through to completion.

Most of this book is based upon unit records and Ninth Air Force records and publications. Much of the documentation pertaining to Group Headquarters came from Colonel William B. Reed (USAF, Retired), who commanded the Group from September 1943 until 20 June 1944 and Brigadier General Russell A. Berg, (USAF, Retired), who commanded the Group from 20 June 1944 to the end of the war. Both of these gentlemen were kind enough to send documents from their personal records and long letters covering their thoughts and recollections about the Group's activities and accomplishments. Additional valuable material pertaining to Group HQ came from Mr. Edgar A. Poe, who served as Assistant Operations Officer for many months before his transfer to the newly organized 363rd Tactical Reconnaissance Group.

The appeal for Squadron records was answered from numerous sources and came in surprising quantities. From Lyon L. Davis, former CO of the 15th Tactical Reconnaissance Squadron, came copies of most of the unit's records and the Squadron photo album. Lt. Colonel James E. Williams (USAF, Retired), who served with the 155th Night Photo Squadron, sent monthly historical reports and the Squadron photo album. Mr. William I. Williams provided the 162nd Tactical Reconnaissance Squadron's records and photos. Colonel Merritt Garner (USAF, Retired), who commanded the 31st Photo Squadron, sent historical records pertaining to the Squadron. Mr. John Florence, CO of the 12th Tactical Reconnaissance Squadron, sent personal files and photos, and these were augmented by microfilm records of the Squadron history provided by Mr. William N. Hess. The late J. B. Woodson of the 33rd Photo Squadron Association sent Squadron records and photos, as did Harold Vaughn, Richard Faulkner and Thomas Myers of the 34th Photo Squadron Association. Bob and Craig Balcomb have contributed photos and documents pertaining to the 30th Photo Squadron. Additional material pertaining to the 155th Night Photo Squadron was obtained from the Air Force Museum files, thanks to the assistance of Mrs. Vivian White, Miss Katherine Cassidy, and Mr. Tom Brewer. Mr. Philippe Canonne of Tours, France provided invaluable documents and photos pertaining to the fighter bomber attack directed by 155th Night Photo Squadron aircraft that resulted in the defeat and surrender of a German Army at Chateauroux, France in September 1944.

Personal diaries and journals were provided by several former pilots, and these documents provide an excellent insight into the day to day life of the 10th PRG. Special thanks must go to Mr. Fred Trenner, Mr. John Miefert, Major Haylon R. Wood (USAF, Retired), Mr. John H. Hoefker, Lt. Colonel Clyde B. East (USAF, Retired), Colonel Edward Bishop (USAF, Retired), and Colonel Rufus Woody (USAF, Retired) for allowing me to quote from these documents.

A special part of this book is the photographs, about 95 percent of which were provided by veterans of the 10th Photo Reconnaissance Group, who dug into their albums and old footlockers in order to help. Because of their efforts it is possible to provide an excellent pictorial history of the life and times of the 10th Photo Reconnaissance Group.

Finally I must express my appreciation to a number of people who helped in the production of this book through their technical assistance. Mr. J. Griffin Murphey and Mr. Samuel L. Sox, Jr. spent many hours copying and processing photos for use in this book. Mr. Ted Damick has been extremely helpful in providing serial numbers for many of the Group's aircraft, and artist Tom Tullis did a magnificent job with the color profiles contained in this volume. Mr. James V. Crow again came through with some critical new photos which enhance the photo coverage within the book. Mr. Bill Hess has assisted in numerous ways to include photos, documents, and valued advice based on his many years of experience as an aviation author. Finally I must express my deepest appreciation to my wife, Mary, who has spent endless hours proofreading this manuscript, and to the late Joseph H. Longfellow for his dedicated assistance in this project.

CONTRIBUTORS

Kinniard Allen, Robert Anderson, Charlie Arrington, Eugene Balachowski, Craig Balcomb, Robert Balcomb, Dr.William Barone, Carl Barton, Nick Beale, Russell A. Berg, Edward L. Bishop, Walter Campbell, Leon Canady, Philippe Canonne, Amos Christianson, James Collins, Wendell Conard, Joseph Conroy, James F. Cooper, Mrs. Mike Crevar, James V. Crow, William O. Davenport, Chris Davis, Lyon L. Davis, Robert Dawson, Eugene Demaris, Lang Dickinson, Jack Dingle, Clyde B. East, Alfons Eck, Richard Edgerton, Hal Edwards, William H. Edwards, M. Leo Elliott, John R. Ellis, William Ennis, Jeff Ethell, Richard Faulkner, Mrs. Alma Fette, John Florence, Albert O. Frick, William R. Gardner, Merritt G. Garner, Raymond Gaudette, Carl Giesler, Fairfield Goodale, Dale Goodermote, Lonnie Grisham, Howard Hadden, James E. Harvey, William N. Hess, Richard Hibbert, John H. Hoefker, A. Cliff Holm, Newton E. Jarrard, E. L. Kenney, Frank Khare, Chuck Kinyon, Victor Krasnickas, Edward Lamir, Leland A. Larson, Henry B. Lewis, Mrs. James Lichtenwalner, Richard Linehan, Robert C. Little, William Long, Joseph Luplow, Donald Lynch, Cliff Mackie, Chester Mason, Howard Martin, Edmund Maxwell, Richard McFadden, John F. Miefert, Thomas H. Milner, Earl Miner, Thomas Myers, Stanley Newman, E. J O'Brien, Charles Ochs, Garry Pape, Wayne S. Patrick, Franklin Pfieffer, E. A. "Jack" Poe, Lawrence "Pete" Posey, Robert Raymond, Charles F. Read, Merlin L. Reed, William B. Reed, Fred H. Remian, Marvin Renner, Harold Robertson, Ben Rosen, Charles Rowland, Ken Rust, Ernest Schonard, Dale Shimon, Robert Shively, Robert T. Simpson IV, Russell Stelle, John Stilla, William L. Swisher, Fred Territti, John Tillett, E. B. Travis, Fred J. Trenner, Theodore Trulson, Harry S. Utley, Pete Valentine, Harold Vaughn, Lloyd Verket, Elmer Wagner, Mrs. Mary Waits, Merle Wallen, Byrne Warren, Arthur Wiedenbein, James E. Williams, William I.Williams, Stewart A. Wilson, Haylon R. Wood, Gordon H. Woodrow, Rufus Woody, Ralph Woolner, and Richard Youll.

FOREWORD

Russell A. Berg
Brigadier General, USAF (Retired)
Commanding Officer, 10th Photo Reconnaissance Group
June 1944-May 1945

I appreciate the opportunity to introduce Tom Ivie's history of the 10th Photo Reconnaissance Group. It is an excellent presentation about the mission of tactical reconnaissance, and about the fine young pilots who flew these hazardous combat missions. I have always been very pleased and proud to answer the question "...*and what did you do in World War Two?*" My prideful answer is: "*I was the Commanding Officer of the 10th Photo Reconnaissance Group.*"

(credit: Robert Dawson)

The Group's primary combat mission was photographic and visual reconnaissance support for the XIX Tactical Air Command activities during the period February-July 1944. Shortly after I assumed command in late June 1944, the Group was given the mission of providing aerial reconnaissance support for General George S. Patton's Third Army as it smashed its way across France and into Germany. General Patton was quick to recognize the importance of tactical reconnaissance and throughout the war wrote numerous letters of appreciation to the 10th PRG for its contributions to the Third Army's campaign. I thank all of the personnel for their participation and personal contributions to the 10th PRG's success in carrying out this important mission.

The following presentation of our story is interesting and worthwhile reading for all aviation enthusiasts.

Russell A. Berg

1

"EQUAL TO THE TASK"

The Early Years: September 1941 to February 1944

After a combat tour in North Africa that included a major role in the Ploesti oilfield raids, the American Ninth Air Force was re-born in England as a tactical air force. It was equipped with B-26 and A-20 bombers, P-47 and P-38 fighters, and F-4/5 and F-6 (photo-recon versions of the P-38 and P-51). The time was October 1943 and its initial missions were in support of Operation Pointblank, which called for the destruction of German aircraft, ball bearing, and munitions factories. While the heavy bombers of the Eighth Air Force struck targets deep in Germany, the Ninth Air Force's medium bombers hit targets in occupied Europe. Simultaneously, its bomber, fighter, reconnaissance, and troop carrier groups trained hard for their new role as a tactical air force.

In December 1943 the Ninth Air Force was integrated into the Allied Expeditionary Air Force commanded by Air Marshal, Sir Trafford Leigh-Mallory. The AEAF was composed of all British and American tactical air force units that would be supporting Operation Overlord, the invasion of occupied Europe. At this time the Ninth Air Force had only one reconnaissance group, the 67th Tactical Reconnaissance Group, to support its operations. As D-Day planning progressed it became obvious that the requirements for aerial reconnaissance would far exceed the capabilities of the 67th TRG, and Ninth Air Force requested an additional reconnaissance group. The request was quickly approved and in February 1944 the 10th Photographic Group (Reconnaissance), commanded by Colonel William B. Reed, arrived in England from Key Field, Mississippi and set up operations at Chalgrove.

On paper the 10th Photo Recon Group was a newly activated unit, but actually its lineage can be traced back to the 73rd Observation Group. The 73rd OG was activated on 1 September 1941 in Harrisburg, Pennsylvania with Major Edgar Scattergood as acting commanding officer. Its stay in Harrisburg was a short one, however, and in November 1941, the 73rd OG was reassigned to Godman Field, Fort Knox, Kentucky and placed under the command of Lieutenant Colonel John C. Kennedy.

Headquarters, 73rd Observation Group moved to Godman Field on 25 November 1941 and its assigned squadrons were: 12th Observation Squadron, Godman Field, Kentucky; 16th Observation Squadron, Lawson Field, Georgia; 22nd Observation Squadron, DeRidder Army Air Base, Louisiana; 91st Observation Squadron, Wheeler-Sack Field, Pine Camp, New York.

Although each of its squadrons was already an operational unit and flying training missions at their respective bases, the 73rd OG Headquarters was still a skeleton crew and directed most of its efforts toward recruiting. One of the first men recruited by the 73rd was Louis Stapp of nearby Louisville, Kentucky who enlisted on an impulse one day while making a delivery to Ft. Knox. After a few days Stapp began to wonder if he had made a big mistake since the 73rd had no supplies, little equipment, and very little for him to do. In an effort to

The 10th PRG unit crest designed by Louis Stapp. The title of "Argus Watching Over the World" and the motto 'Ceaseless Watch' symbolized the ever vigilant eyes of the observation air crews. (*credit: Air Force Museum*)

keep busy Pvt. Stapp decided to put his artistic talents to use by performing a service that would have lasting significance to the 73rd Observation Group and its successor, the 10th Photo Reconnaissance Group. He designed the Unit Crest of "Argus Watching Over the World" and gave the 73rd its motto of "Ceaseless Watch".

The Japanese attack on Pearl Harbor on 7 December 1941, provided the impetus to get the 73rd's organization and training activities into high gear. On 11 December 1941 nine officers and 20 enlisted men were transferred to HQ 73rd OG from the 12th Observation Squadron to form the staff and Headquarters Squadron. With his headquarters staff now in place, Lieutenant Colonel Kennedy drew up a Group training schedule for his scattered squadrons and the 73rd OG was finally gearing itself to war-time conditions.

Training missions flown by the 91st Observation Squadron for several weeks following the Japanese attack on Pearl Harbor took on an operational flavor. From its base in Pine Camp, New York the 91st OS flew missions along the border between New York and Canada and photographed any possible landing sites that could be used by enemy aircraft. The attack on Pearl Harbor had smashed forever the idea that an ocean barrier would prevent an attack on the United States.

As the 91st undertook these missions in its O-46 and O-47 observation aircraft it soon became obvious that the squadron's worst enemy was the cold, snowy New York weather, and it cost the squadron one of its few aircraft. Newton E. Jarrard, who was assigned as an aerial observer recalled that fateful flight: "We all thought someone was crazy because we knew of no German aircraft that could fly the ocean while laden with

A Douglas O-46A (later RO-46A) of the 91st Observation Squadron. This squadron was assigned to the 73rd Observation Group from September 1941 to June 1943 (credit: Air Force Museum)

summer of 1942 the squadron was sent to Panama City, Florida for flexible gunnery training, and in August 1942 it joined the remainder of the 73rd Observation Group at Godman Field, Kentucky.

By the time the 91st arrived at Godman Field several organizational changes had been made. The Group was now commanded by Colonel Robert M. Lee and consisted of Headquarters, 73rd OG; the 15th Observation Squadron, the 28th Observation Squadron and the 91st Observation Squadron, all of which were at Godman Field.

The training missions recorded in the 15th Observation Squadron's historical reports are typical of the type of training the 73rd OG undertook during the spring and summer of 1942. These missions supported the armored divisions stationed at Ft. Knox, Kentucky and consisted of strafing, bombing, aerial reconnaissance, and photography. In July 1942 the 15th OS was sent to Louisiana to participate in maneuvers. During the maneuvers the squadron flew traditional pre-war battlefield observation missions over the armies engaged below. Its pilots carried out their assignments in the finest tradition of observation crews as they lumbered along in their slow and clumsy "O-birds," but a number of the pilots had already begun to question these tactics in a modern war.

When the 15th OS returned to Godman Field in September 1942, its personnel noticed the first indication of a welcome change. P-51A fighters and A-20 light bombers sat on the tarmac and the mere presence of these aircraft immediately increased morale within the squadron.

The arrival of modern aircraft signaled the beginning of fundamental changes in the reconnaissance doctrines of the United States Army Air Force. Reports filtering in from the campaign in North Africa made the USAAF command finally realize that its observation tactics and aircraft were woefully out of date. It was now time for some real changes to be made. The first order of business was a total reorganization of observation units, and in doing so the USAAF followed the Royal Air Force's example. Observation units were divided into three distinct categories: liaison squadrons using light aircraft such as Piper L-4s and Stinson L-5s for artillery spotting and courier

equipment necessary to land and set up operations from the North American continent. Nevertheless, we set about scheduling the mission and on a cold overcast day we took off to make our photo run. Our crew was assigned to photograph the area around Lake Placid and we were out of radio range when the recall message was sent out from our field. We had just finished photographing several civilian fields and were heading toward Lake Placid when the snowstorm hit and forced us down to about 50 feet altitude. At this time we were hopelessly lost and finally the pilot announced that we were down to less than five minutes of fuel. We decided to belly it on a big pasture when the pilot spotted a highway and tried a wheels-down landing. The O-47 was rolling down the highway when we suddenly pulled up and passed over an oncoming automobile and a tree, then we lost power again and landed on the highway. The O-47 was still rolling at about 50 miles per hour when we came to a bend in the road, clipped about three feet off the left wing and washed out the plane against a telephone pole. Needless to say our commanding officer was quite upset with us since we had reduced his O-47 inventory by 50 percent, and had no surviving photos to show for our efforts."

After these needless photo missions were completed the 91st OS began training missions consisting of air-to-ground communication, photography, and navigation. During the

Colonel Robert M. Lee (center) commanded the 73rd Observation Group during the period February to December 1942 and was instrumental in its development. (credit: Lyon L. Davis)

When the 15th Observation Squadron was detailed to the Louisiana Maneuvers during the summer of 1942, its crews were still flying the obsolescent North American O-47 as depicted in this photograph.
(credit: Air Force Museum)

The report filed by the historian of the 15th Reconnaissance Squadron provides an interesting look at the activities of the squadron during the period 26 June-25 July 1943. Excerpts from the report noted: *"During the month the squadron provided the ground forces participating with air support in the form of visual and photographic reconnaissance and a few bombing and strafing attacks. It operated independently, receiving mission assignments from and reporting directly to the air support party. Squadron Operations (S-3) planned and directed the missions. Squadron S-2 (Intelligence) briefed and interrogated the pilots, and the communications section kept open the channels of communication via teletype and radio.*

flights; tactical reconnaissance squadrons using armed fighter aircraft on high-speed, low-level visual or photo missions; and photo squadrons using unarmed fighter or light bomber aircraft on high-altitude photo missions.

This new look began to take shape within the 73rd OG during the spring of 1943. In March 1943 the 15th and 91st Observation Squadrons were re-equipped with P-39s, the 28th Observation Squadron with A-20s and the new 14th Liaison Squadron received Piper L-4s. On 9 April 1943, the 73rd Observation Group was redesignated as the 73rd Reconnaissance Group. The 15th and 91st became Reconnaissance Squadrons (Fighter), and the 28th became a Reconnaissance Squadron (Bomber).

During April, May, and June 1943 the 73rd Reconnaissance Group and its squadrons supported the armored divisions based at Ft. Knox, Kentucky and flew what were termed "co-operative" missions. The 15th RS, for example, flew probing and strafing missions behind "enemy" lines. The pace was fast and furious. Three of the 15th's pilots, including its commanding officer, Captain James Kaden, were killed during this phase of the training.

During the summer and fall of 1943 the 73rd Reconnaissance Group participated in the Tennessee Maneuvers and its squadrons operated from airfields located at Bowling Green, Kentucky and Camp Campbell, Kentucky. During the maneuvers many of the newly developed reconnaissance concepts were tested while the 73rd supported the 101st Airborne Division.

...This simulated warfare taught the pilots and the operations, intelligence, and communications sections many valuable lessons in the conduct and operations of tactical reconnaissance, a new conception of its importance, and a proper respect for the necessity of speed, accuracy, efficiency, and co-ordination.

...As many as 15 missions were flown in a single day. The squadron proved equal to the task. Pilots and ground crews performed their duties most competently. Much important information was obtained for the ground forces, and at critical moments sleek P-39s swooped down to bomb and strafe "enemy" positions. The efficiency of the squadron

The transition from the lumbering "O-birds" to modern fighters did not always go smoothly, as seen in this photograph of one of the 15th Reconnaissance Squadron's first P-51As after a hard landing.
(credit: Joe Conroy)

Lieutenant Chester Mason's Bell P-39N Airacobra, complete with nose art, awaits its next mission from Bowling Green, Kentucky during the Tennessee Maneuvers. This photograph was taken in July 1943. (*credit: L. C. "Pete" Posey*)

impressed the Air Support Command and the ground force commanders."

By August 1943 the redefinition of the tactical reconnaissance mission led to another re-designation. The 73rd was now known as the 73rd Tactical Reconnaissance Group and was composed of the 15th, 28th and 152nd Tactical Reconnaissance Squadrons, all flying P-39s or P-40s. At about the same time the first training manual for *"Advanced Fighter Reconnaissance Training"* developed by Major William B. Reed, who assumed command of the 73rd TRG in September 1943, was released and put into use. One of the prime points of emphasis in the manual's introduction was the qualifications demanded of a tactical reconnaissance pilot. It stated: *"Fighter Reconnaissance pilots must be thoroughly impressed with the fact that they are fighter trained as well as reconnaissance trained and must be capable of performing their duties in both roles in an excellent manner. Pilots must not*

Lieutenant Colonel William B. Reed, CO of the 73rd Reconnaissance Group, is pictured hard at work in his field headquarters at Berry Field, Tennessee during the latter stages of the Tennessee Maneuvers. (*credit: Newton E. Jarrard*)

only develop and perfect their reconnaissance skill, accuracy, speed in observing, but they must also maintain, at a high level, the fighter tactics and techniques with which they were primarily indoctrinated when they graduated from Fighter Command School. An excellent fighter reconnaissance crew by virtue of its additional training skills and techniques will be, in general, equal to a superior fighter crew that had only fighter training."

In addition to the development of tactical reconnaissance tactics, the 73rd TRG also tested night photo reconnaissance during the Tennessee Maneuvers. Dr. Harold Edgerton, inventor of the flash unit, brought an example of his "Edgerton Lamp" to the maneuver area and mounted it in an A-20. The experimental night missions demonstrated that many good photos could be produced using this technique, but there were still some major problems to be resolved. The tests, however, did show sufficient promise to warrant a recommendation that work must be continued so the lamp could go into operational service. Night missions using the standard M-46 flash bombs were also flown during this period, but were

RIGHT: Dr. Harold Edgerton of the Massachusetts Institute of Technology, inventor of the Edgerton Lamp used so successfully by the 155th NPS in 1944-45. (*credit: James E. Williams*)

BELOW: During its modernization period at Godman Field, Kentucky during the fall of 1942, the 15th OS also received A-20 Havocs into its inventory. (*credit: Lyon L. Davis*)

LEFT: Mission ahead: Lieutenant "Pete" Posey a conducts pre-flight check of his P-39 prior to heading out over "enemy" territory. (*credit: L. C. "Pete" Posey*)

RIGHT: As a P-39 of the 15th Reconnaissance Squadron lifts off, two other P-39s wait in line for their turn. The bands visible on the wings are temporary war-game markings depicting which side the squadron was on. (*credit: Lyon L. Davis*)

LEFT: An excellent photograph of a pontoon bridge over the Ohio River taken by a pilot of the 15th Reconnaissance Squadron on 5 August 1943 during the Tennessee Maneuvers. (*credit: Robert Anderson*)

A photograph of interest to modelers: even those who apply markings to the real thing sometimes make mistakes! Note the upside-down national insignia on this 15th Reconnaissance Squadron P-51A.
(*credit: Newton E. Jarrard*)

discontinued after a "dud" flash bomb hit and killed a cow standing in its pasture.

A third experiment performed by the 73rd TRG was the testing of some of the early strip cameras and evaluating their potential, a concept which was later to play a big role in the preparations for the invasion of Normandy.

At the end of the Tennessee Maneuvers, Headquarters, 73rd TRG and its sole remaining squadron, the 15th TRS, were reassigned to Key Field, Meridian, Mississippi for more training. During October 1943 the 15th TAC R Squadron received alert orders for overseas movement and reassignment to the 67th Tactical Reconnaissance Group in England.

After the departure of the 15th TAC R Squadron in December 1943, Colonel Reed received notice that Headquarters, 73rd TRG would be disbanded and its personnel reassigned to other commands. This decision did not sit well with Colonel Reed and on 30 December 1943 he headed to Washington D.C. to try to undo it. After two days of pounding on doors, he was given an audience with the Deputy Chief of Staff for Operations. At the outset of the meeting Colonel Reed was informed that none of the USAAF Theaters of Operation had stated a need for anything other than squadron-size units and that the 73rd TRG was excess to the needs of the Service. Bill Reed later recalled: "The meeting was going nowhere until I expounded on the super qualifications of the 73rd as an organization which, with minimum training, could effectively command anything from a heavy bomb group to a photo group. The Deputy Chief responded, '*Did you say photo group?*' I nodded and he said, '*I think we've got a request for a photo group headquarters, I'll check it out and let you know tomorrow.*' The request was verified and I rushed back to Key Field to let everybody know that we were alive and well as the 10th Photo Reconnaissance Group."

After a brief training program at Will Rogers Field, Oklahoma, the 10th PRG headquarters personnel packed up and departed on 24 January 1944 for England and an assignment to the Ninth Air Force. Nearly one month later, on 21 February 1944, the 10th Photo Reconnaissance Group opened for business at Station 465, Chalgrove in Oxfordshire, England, with the 30th Photo Squadron as its first assigned unit.

January 1944, Colonel Bill Reed poses with his family at Key Field, Mississippi prior to heading to England with his 10th PRG staff.
(*credit: William B. Reed*)

2

"DICING"
Prelude to Invasion: February 1944 to D-Day

The situation in the Allied camp at the time of the 10th Photo Reconnaissance Group's arrival in England can best be described, from both planning and operational standpoints, as extremely busy. The driving force behind this activity was the arrival of General Dwight D. Eisenhower, who had returned from the Mediterranean Theater of Operations, to assume his new position as Supreme Commander of the Allied invasion forces. The timetable called for the invasion of occupied Europe during the spring and summer of 1944 and, if the invasion was to be a success, many pre-invasion objectives had to be met.

First and foremost, the *Luftwaffe* and the industrial infrastructure that fed the German war machine would have to be destroyed. To accomplish this mandatory objective the US Army Air Forces in Europe underwent a major reorganization. This included the return of the Ninth Air Force to England (to be retrained as a tactical air force), the establishment of the Fifteenth Air Force in Italy, and a restructuring of command within the Eighth Air Force. Along with this reorganization came the implementation of the combined bomber offensive which would provide round-the-clock attacks upon the Third Reich by bombers of the USAAF and the Royal Air Force.

General H.H. Arnold, the commanding general of all American Air Forces, emphasized the need to eliminate the *Luftwaffe* as a prerequisite to invasion by issuing this aggressive order to his commanders in the field: "*This is a must, destroy the enemy air forces wherever you find them, in the air, on the ground, and in the factories.*"

To bolster the morale of the long-suffering Eighth Air Force bomber groups, General Arnold also promised new long-range fighters that could escort the bombers to their targets and back. The need for these long-range fighters was paramount because the Eighth Air Force had suffered heavy losses during the raids on Schweinfurt and other major targets the previous year. So disastrous were these losses that daylight raids deep into Germany had to be suspended until the new fighters became operational late in 1943 and early 1944. With the arrival of the new P-51 Mustang, and improved fuel systems for the P-47s and P-38s, the Eighth Air Force was now ready to resume its offensive.

By February 1944 the Eighth Air Force was dispatching massive formations of escorted bombers against industrial targets deep in Germany and delivered a devastating blow to German industry during the period of 20-25 February 1944. During the so-called "Big Week," Allied bombers dropped over 20,000 tons of explosives on aircraft factories

V-1 site in France photographed by Lt. John F. Hickman of the 107th TRS during Operation Pointblank. (*credit: John F. Hickman*)

and related targets, setting back Germany's fighter production by two months. Approximately 600 German aircraft were destroyed in air-to-air combat or in the wrecked factories.

While the Eighth Air Force was hitting strategic targets, the Ninth Air Force was deeply committed to attacking Pointblank and Crossbow targets (V-1 flying-bomb sites) in France and the Low Countries. Pointblank targets included the French railroads, rail facilities and bridges, industrial facilities and airfields in the occupied countries, as well as German coastal defenses and radar systems.

The existing reconnaissance units in England also played a major role in these air assaults by providing target photos and then following up with battle damage assessment photos taken immediately after the raid. This, in itself, was enough to keep them busy but, in addition to

Before the arrival of the 10th PRG in England, the 67th Tactical Reconnaissance Group carried the heavy burden of conducting pre-invasion reconnaissance for the Ninth Air Force. This F-6B Mustang was assigned to its 107th TRS. (*credit: Air Force Museum*)

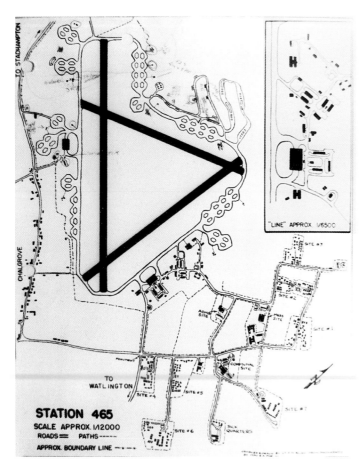

Station 465, Chalgrove, Oxfordshire, England was the 10th PRG's base between February and August 1944. (*credit: William B. Reed*)

these missions, the Ninth Air Force's 67th Tactical Reconnaissance Group was also required to provide coverage of the proposed invasion beaches. Needless to say, the 67th TRG was stretched to its limits and the arrival of the 10th Photo Reconnaissance Group was a welcome relief.

The 30th Photo Squadron, commanded by Captain Richard Leghorn, arrived at Chalgrove on 1 February 1944 and this "orphan" squadron immediately began its preparations for combat. It was a far from easy job. Tools and equipment were in short supply or non-existent, and all sections had to beg, borrow, or "mid-night requisition" supplies to get the Squadron operational. In an effort to accelerate the Squadron's preparations, Captain Leghorn also dispatched four of his officers to the 3rd PRG based in Italy to get some first-hand information about tactics and procedures used in combat. Training missions began as aircraft became available and the 30th PS suffered its first loss on 24 February 1944 when Lt. Howard Struble was killed when his F-5 crashed at Crossway Hard Farm, Southwick.

By the time Headquarters, 10th PRG arrived at Chalgrove on 21 February 1944 the 30th Photo Squadron had solved most of its problems and was ready to begin operations. Four days later Colonel William B. Reed, anxious to end two and a half years of training, declared the Squadron combat ready.

The 30th Photo Squadron's first mission was flown on 25 February 1944 by Captain Leghorn, who successfully photographed the airfields at Querqueville and Maupertus on the Cherbourg Peninsula. The Squadron's second mission, flown 29 February by Captain William Mitchell, failed as both target areas were completely obscured by 10/10th cloud cover.

In March 1944, Ninth Air Force Bomber Command shifted its target priorities and placed German airfields, marshaling yards, and boat pens along the Channel coast at the top of the list. With this increase in activity the 10th PRG would be kept quite busy providing bomb damage assessment photos of these targets and monitoring the activities of German airfields. During the first two weeks of

ABOVE: Captain William Mitchell of the 30th PS. (*credit: Bob and Craig Balcomb*)

RIGHT: During the spring of 1944, actor James Cagney visited Chalgrove. In this photograph Colonel Bill Reed is giving Cagney a close look at the controls of a 30th PS F-5 Lightning. (*credit: William B. Reed*)

B-26s of the 386th Bomb Group heading for occupied Europe to mount strikes on German rail targets. (*USAF*)

photographed the port of Cherbourg and two airfields on the peninsula.

By April 1944 the effects of Operation Pointblank were beginning to show. The *Luftwaffe* had withdrawn the majority of its fighter units from France and the Low Countries, and those that stayed moved to bases deeper in France. Because of the *Luftwaffe*'s re-deployment, the Ninth Air Force's bombers and reconnaissance aircraft could now proceed in earnest with their task of preparing the way for invasion.

the month the Squadron flew photo missions to German installations along the French and Belgian coasts. The first six sorties of the month were flown on the 2nd and 3rd by Lts. Russell Miller, Charles Rudel, Donald Thompson, Chapman Bone, and Lester Sarvik who successfully photographed port facilities and airfields from Calais to Cherbourg. Seven further missions of this type were flown on 6 and 8 March, and all successfully brought back photos of similar targets.

After standing down for a week, the 30th PS returned to the Continent on 15 March to begin a series of bomb damage assessment missions following operations flown by Ninth Bomber Command against marshaling yards, locomotive works and other targets along the French-Belgian border. To carry out its bomb damage assessment missions the Squadron's pilots would appear over the target within 30 minutes of the attack and photograph the results of the attack for first phase interpretation. One of these missions occurred on 20 March 1944 when 124 B-26s of the 386th, 387th, 344th, and 391st Bomb Groups heavily damaged the Creil marshaling yards, several factories and a locomotive works. Three pilots from the 30th PS, Lts. Donald Thompson, Donald Martin, and Henry Wallaert, accompanied the bombers and Lt. Martin brought back some excellent photos of the damage. A follow-up raid against the Creil marshaling yards and the German air base at Beaumont-le-Roger was carried out on 23 March and again the 30th PS followed up with successful photo missions over the target areas.

The most notable event of 23 March 1944, however was the arrival of the 31st Photo Squadron commanded by Major Rudolph Walters. The 31st's arrival could not have been more timely as the demand for photographic information was increasing daily and to illustrate the point, Major Walters was directed to have his squadron ready for operations within three weeks.

While the 31st Photo Squadron readied itself for combat missions, the 30th PS continued its coverage of assigned targets. The month of March was closed out by two successful missions on 31 March. Colonel Bill Reed mapped a portion of the Cherbourg Peninsula while his Assistant Operations Officer, Major Edgar A. "Jack" Poe,

During April 1944 the 10th PRG continued its bomb damage assessment missions, and also took on some important new assignments. The new work included mapping of large areas of the Continent, and surveillance of 36 primary and secondary enemy airfields.

Weather had an adverse effect on operations during the first week of April; only two of six missions flown were successful and several others were cancelled. Finally on 10 April the weather cleared and 16 missions were flown, 13 of which were successful. Included in the day's combat operations was the first by the newly arrived 31st Photo Squadron. The 31st's inaugural mission was flown by Major

Major Rudolph Walters, CO of the 31st PS. In this photograph, taken in December 1944, Walters (center) has just been presented the Silver Star, by General O. P. Weyland (left). (*credit: Robert Dawson*)

ABOVE: A very pleased Major Don Hayes, CO of the 34th PS, after returning from his and the Squadron's first combat mission on 19 April 1944. (*credit: Ben Rosen*)

ABOVE: Major Leon McCurdy, CO of the 33rd PS. McCurdy flew his squadron's first mission on 23 May 1944. (*credit: J. B. Woodson*)

Walters who, after finding his primary targets covered by cloud, continued on to his secondary targets and brought back excellent photos.

The missions of 18 April 1944 were a masterful accomplishment for the 10th PRG, especially when considering it had been flying operationally only for two months. On that day, five 30th PS pilots, Lts. Max Spenser, Charles Rudel, Lyman Simpson, Henry Wallaert, and Charles Wright, flew their F-5s to an altitude of 30,000 ft over Holland and mapped three-quarters of the country in just 45 minutes – a remarkable feat which indicated that the 10th Photo Reconnaissance Group was rapidly coming of age.

On 19 April the Group's third squadron, the 34th Photo Squadron, which had arrived at Chalgrove on 30 March, flew its first mission. It was flown by the Squadron commander, Major Don Hayes, who successfully photographed the airfields at Maupertus and Querqueville on the Cherbourg Peninsula. With three squadrons now operational the 10th Photo Recon Group was able to send its aircraft far and wide over the Continent and covered targets in Normandy, Brittany, Loire, Belgium, and even to Metz, a heavily defended communications center near the German border.

During the final week of April 1944 the Group's fourth and final F-5 squadron, the 33rd Photo Squadron, under the command of Major Leon McCurdy, arrived at Chalgrove.

With the arrival of the 33rd a new phase of the Group's mission was initiated. D Flight of the 33rd was immediately put on detached service with the 423rd Night Fighter Squadron and began training in night photo reconnaissance. Within a few weeks the unit was redesignated as the 155th Night Photo Reconnaissance Squadron.

With three squadrons now operational, the 10th PRG was able to dispatch 170 missions during the month of April. Of that total 135 were carried out successfully, and in doing so the 10th PRG was able to map large portions of France, Belgium, and Holland for General Eisenhower's planners.

In addition to the missions over the continent of Europe, the 31st PS was assigned a list of locations in England to photograph for the Air Ministry. These photos were used to aid in the study of defense installations. In carrying out these missions the Squadron suffered its first loss when Lt. William Haywood crashed in bad weather near Shrewsbury. The 34th PS also suffered its first loss when Lt. Ralph T. Cameron was killed during a training mission on 14 April.

While the squadrons of the 10th Photo Reconnaissance Group continued flying their high-altitude operational and training missions, Colonel Reed and several members of his staff departed for Italy for a visit to Colonel Karl Polifka and his 3rd Photo Group. While there, Colonel Reed, Lieutenant Colonel Richard Hibbert, (Group S-2).

Major Jack Dingle poses with his *flak*-damaged F-5 after his "dicing" mission in Italy, April 1944. (*credit: Jack Dingle*)

demonstrated the low-level and "dicing" missions they had been flying in Italy and expounded on their potential for use in the pre-invasion work by the 10th PRG. While in Italy Colonel Reed and Major Dingle flew some of these low-level missions, and Dingle was almost lost in the Anzio area while flying what was actually the 10th's first "dicing" mission. His F-5 was hit several times by *flak*, one piece of which tore a gaping hole in his left rudder and sent him limping back to base.

Armed with the requirements needed to enable his pilots to get detailed photos of German beach defenses along the Normandy coast, Colonel Reed and his party headed back to Chalgrove. Shortly after his return his squadron commanders were briefed about the new missions they would be flying and plans were made for the Group's introduction to "dicing." One can well imagine the surprise on the faces of pilots who were told when they began operations back in February and March that they "…might have to operate as low as 29,000 feet," and were now being told that they would soon be making runs over the heavily defended areas of Normandy at 50 feet!

and Major Jack Dingle, (Group S-3), were given a briefing and training on a type of mission that was a far cry from what they were used to. The concept that Colonel Polifka taught was an eye-opener for the visitors. Here, instead of flying high-altitude missions of 29,000 to 35,000 ft, they would soon be flying low-level missions that had been developed by the 3rd Photo Group. Colonel Polifka

The 10th PRG would be flying a combination of high-altitude and "dicing" missions during the weeks to come because photos of both types were needed critically by the Invasion Planners. In early May 1944, however, the 21st Army Group was pleading for low-level photos of the

LEFT: The first "dicing" mission over the Normandy coastline was flown on 6 May 1944 by Lieutenant Al Lanker in an F-5A Lightning named *The Outlaw*. This aircraft, s/n 42-12778, was named after the movie starring Jane Russell. (*credit: Rufus Woody*)

BELOW: A close-up of the artwork adorning Lt.. Lanker's F-5A. (*credit: William K. Moher via Jim Crow*)

proposed invasion beaches that would show the barriers, mines, and other beach obstacles in detail.

By the beginning of May the 10th PRG was fully trained and prepared for bringing back low-level photos, and on 6 May Lt. Albert Lanker of the 31st PS was chosen to fly the first dicing mission. The Squadron diary described the mission: *"On the afternoon of May 6, he took off with the prayers and good wishes of every man in the* Squadron *riding with him. This was his third mission, and Lt. Lanker was to photograph a strip of beach twenty miles long from Le Tréport to Berck-sur-Mer. Because missions of this type have always been considered suicidal by most recce pilots Lt. Lanker was somewhat nervous and apprehensive as he lifted his F-5 off the runway at Chalgrove and headed toward the Channel. At Dungeness he was flying at fifty feet above the trees when he circled his aircraft and shot across the Channel ten to fifteen feet above the waves. Near Berck-sur-Mer Lt. Lanker turned around a sand dune to lessen his possibilities of being a target (photos later revealed the sand dune to be an enemy gun emplacement), and gaining speed in*

RIGHT: As Lanker makes his low-level pass over Normandy his aircraft casts a perfect shadow of itself upon the beach. (*credit: Edgar A. "Jack" Poe*)

BELOW: Beach obstacles photographed by Lanker's "dicing" camera in the nose of his F-5A. Just visible are German workers fleeing as he approaches. (*credit: Edgar A. "Jack" Poe*)

a short dive, started his photo run. At this point Lt. Lanker said his nervousness left him and he began to enjoy himself immensely. During the four minutes his cameras were operating he encountered five groups of workmen building defenses on the beach, and later related, 'I headed straight for every group just to watch them scatter and roll. They were completely surprised – didn't see me until I was almost on top of them'. Near the end of his run he scaled a cliff with his wingtip six feet from the top, and a German soldier fired a rifle at him. This was the only opposition he encountered during the entire mission. When Lanker returned and landed his aircraft he was met and cheered and congratulated by members of the 10th PRG headquarters and the 31st Squadron alike."

ABOVE: After returning from his 19 May 1944 "dicing" mission, Lt. Rufus Woody poses for the photographers in his F-5B *Alice*. (*credit: Rufus Woody*)

BELOW: The only fatality incurred during the pre-Invasion "dicing" missions was Lieutenant Fred Hayes of the 31st PS who disappeared on 7 May 1944. His aircraft was last seen as it crossed the English coastline and headed out over the Channel. (*credit: Rufus Woody*)

The jubilation was certainly warranted because Lt. Lanker's photos showed the beach defenses in great detail, and workmen ducking to escape the aircraft which must have seemed to be heading straight for them. His "dicing" mission was so successful that the 10th PRG scheduled two more for the next day. On 7 May 1944 the unit dispatched 25 missions; only ten of them were successful, and two pilots were lost. One of the losses was Lt. Lloyd Haslup of the 34th PS who was lost on a conventional photo mission over Châteaudun airfield, and the second was Lt. Fred Hayes of the 31st PS. Lt. Hayes was lost while attempting a "dicing" mission. After leaving the English coastline Hayes and his aircraft simply vanished and he was never heard from again. Captain William Mitchell of the 30th PS, who took off at the same time as Hayes, successfully completed his "dicing" run along the coastline stretching from Dunkirk to Ostend, Belgium.

During the period 8-15 May the Group's pilots carried out high-altitude missions which included photographing marshaling yards, airfields, and bridges, and mapping throughout France and Belgium. These missions cost another pilot, when Lt. Richard E. Knickerbocher of the 34th PS was shot down and killed as he was returning from a bomb damage assessment mission to the Aerschot marshaling yards.

No missions were flown from 16-18 May. On 19 May the second series of "dicing" missions were flown, and they covered the planned invasion beaches of Normandy from Ouistreham to St.-Vaast-la-Hogue. Three of the four were successful. They were flown by Lts. Donald F. Thompson of the 30th, Rufus Woody of the 31st, and Garland A. York of the 34th. Lt. Merritt Garner of the 31st was unable to take off with the other three aircraft because of brake trouble. Garner did try to fly his mission but by the time he arrived at his assigned area the Germans had been alerted and put up a hail of *flak* so intense he could not make his photo run.

Lieutenant York's assignment was to cover the area of beaches that later became famous as "Omaha" and "Utah" beaches on D-Day. His photos revealed the German "hedgehogs," which were obstacles made from steel beams and designed to rip the bottom out of landing barges, sloped ramps designed to overturn the barges, and other obstacles that would be invisible at high tide.

Three more "dicing" missions on 20 May were successfully flown by Lts. James Poole and Robert Holbury of the 31st, and Lieutenant Joseph Smith of the 30th. A fourth "dicing" mission, flown by Lieutenant Allen R. Keith of the 34th PS, was nearly foiled by an 'enemy' seagull. Just prior to completing his assigned area of Fécamp to Hequeville, Lieutenant Keith hit the seagull and it crashed through the Plexiglas windshield. Fortunately the bullet-proof glass stopped the bird before it smashed into Keith. In spite of the bloody mess on his windshield, Keith continued his mission and brought back excellent photos of German beach defenses and gun positions along the cliffs above the beaches.

Lts. Holbury and Smith both completed their assigned photo runs without incident, but Lieutenant Poole did not have it so easy. He missed his initial point at St. Valéry-en-Caux and entered the coast at a point approximately five miles west of Dieppe and flew up the coast to a point about three miles west of Boulogne. Through an error in navigation Lieutenant Poole again entered the coast at Boulogne, drew intense ground fire, realized his error and flew away. At Boulogne, however, he was able to turn on

LEFT: Lieutenant Garland A. York of the 34th PS (*credit: 34th PS Assn*)

BELOW: This F-5A, s/n 42-12786, was flown by Lts. Garland A. York and Allen Keith on their respective "dicing" missions of 19 and 20 May. The Lightning carried the name *My Little De-Icer* on the right side of the nose. This photograph shows the aircraft as it appeared during the summer of 1944. (*credit: Ben Rosen*)

Lieutenant Allen Keith, whose life was probably saved by the armored glass in his cockpit when an "enemy" seagull crashed through the windshield, completed his "dicing" run in spite of impaired forward visibility and returned with excellent photographs. (*credit: 34th PS Assn*)

squadron became operational when Major McCurdy flew the 33rd Photo Squadron's first mission on 23 May and successfully photographed his targets.

Of major importance during the closing days of May was a test mission flown by D Flight of the 423rd Night Fighter Squadron. For the test an Edgerton Lamp was mounted in one of the squadron's F-3A (A-20J) Havocs, and its crew returned with good clear photos of the "target area." With this success the night photo crews now had the capability of taking 186 photos as opposed to eight on aircraft using M-46 flash bombs (see Appendix 1).

Thus ended May 1944, a month of monumental achievement for the 10th Photo Reconnaissance Group. With the

his cameras and photograph a short strip of the coast in this area. These missions turned out to be the last pre-invasion "dicing" missions over Normandy. The photos brought back during this series of missions had provided enough detailed pictures of the beach defenses to give Allied commanders a good idea of what their troops would face.

With the successful completion of these important low-level missions, the 10th Photo Reconnaissance Group had proved that after only three months of combat flying, it was second to none. So important were these photos to General Eisenhower and his staff, that Ike and many of the commanders involved in the invasion planning sent glowing letters of appreciation to the 10th PRG, and each pilot that participated received the Distinguished Flying Cross. A few weeks later the 10th PRG received the Distinguished Unit Citation for its remarkable work (see Appendix 2). One other very significant benefit the pilots derived from these missions was the realization that close teamwork with the ground forces paid off in lives saved.

For the remainder of May 1944 the 10th PRG flew its conventional high-altitude missions of bomb damage assessment, airfield surveillance, and mapping. Also during this period the Group's fourth

continued success of its high altitude surveillance missions, the introduction of "dicing" missions, and the final development of improved night photography, the 10th was a well-rounded and well-trained unit in the fullest sense of the word. May, however, would be the last full month that the Group would operate as a strictly photo reconnaissance group. The coming invasion would soon place entirely new demands on all of the Ninth Air Force reconnaissance units.

The ground crew of *My Little De-Icer* pose proudly with their ship which now displays two "dicing" mission markers and one seagull to indicate its victory over the attacking "enemy" bird. (*34th PS Assn*)

LEFT: The ground crew of Lieutenant Woody's F-5 *Alice* pose with their aircraft. C/C M/Sgt. Joe Dziak is in the cockpit while in the foreground is Sgt. Pietka. (*credit: Rufus Woody*)

BELOW: During the summer of 1944 Lieutenant Woody's F-5B, s/n 42-68258, which previously only displayed the name Alice on the left engine cowl, was spiced up a little with this nose art and named *Sweat'Er Out*. (*credit: James Black via Jim Crow*)

LEFT: Major Joe Gillespie (left) and his crew check the Edgerton Lamp mounted in their F-3A prior to the day's mission. (*credit: James Williams*)

LEFT: An F-3A (A-20J) Havoc of the 155th NPS lifts off the runway at Chalgrove and heads toward its target in Europe. The Havoc, designed as a light bomber, also evolved as an excellent platform for the Squadron's nocturnal photo missions. (*credit: J. B. Woodson*)

3

"GET THOSE PHOTOS REGARDLESS OF THE WEATHER"
D-Day and the Aftermath: June to July 1944

While May was a month of accomplishment for the 10th PRG, June was to be a month of both accomplishment and change. These changes would be major and encompass both the command and organizational structure of the 10th Photo Reconnaissance Group.

From an operational standpoint there was an air of great anticipation because it was known that the invasion of Europe must be imminent. This had to be obvious to the reconnaissance pilots who had covered the beach areas of Normandy in May and were now engaged in mapping the Cherbourg Peninsula, and carefully checking bridges, road junctions, and known supply routes throughout Normandy and Brittany.

Finally on 5 June 1944 Colonel Reed received word that the invasion would take place the following day, and that the 423rd Night Fighter Squadron (155th Night Photo Squadron) would have the honor of flying the first mission of D-Day. The Squadron's assignment was to check for any German rail or highway movement along the Cherbourg Peninsula. Shortly before midnight on the night of 5/6 June 1944 four F-3As lifted off the runway at Chalgrove and headed for France. They maintained an altitude of 3,000 ft until reaching the Channel Islands and then climbed to 8000 ft for their target runs. Three of the F-3As, piloted by Lts. Thomas Starmont, Conoly G. Anderson, and Cliff Mackie carried flash bombs, and the fourth, piloted by Lieutenant William Lentscher, carried an Edgerton Lamp. As they approached the target area a heavy undercast was encountered and accurate navigation was hindered. None of the crews had any real experience with the GEE system of navigation, and the three aircraft carrying the flash bombs were unable to carry out their assignment. The fourth aircraft, however, located its targets and utilized its Edgerton Lamp to bring back extremely clear photos of Villedieu-les-Poêles and Coutances. These photos showed no evidence of any German movement, indicating that the *Wehrmacht* was not expecting landings in Normandy.

As the landings in Normandy progressed the 10th PRG's mission was two-fold. Some of its aircraft were sent beyond the invasion area to keep a close watch on bridges and roads that the Germans might use to bring up reinforcements, while others continued the mapping of the Cherbourg Peninsula. By nightfall the pilots of the 10th PRG had flown 63 missions in support of the D-Day landings, and by now had come to realize, with a great deal of pride, that its role in the pre-invasion preparations was a major contribution to its success.

With a foothold established, the Allies continued to pour troops and supplies onto the beaches in preparation

This crew provided proof that the Germans were not aware that the Normandy Invasion was about to take place on the morning of 6 June, and a relieved General Eisenhower subsequently gave the order to "go". From left to right: Lt. William Lentscher (pilot), Lt. Cohn (navigator/photographer) and Sgt. James Willis (gunner). *(credit: James Williams)*

for the breakout from the beaches. In an effort to assist the troops on the ground, the 10th PRG had its aircraft over the front day and night. The importance of this surveillance was emphasized in the mission orders of 8 June in which the Ninth Air Force directed the 10th PRG "*...to get those photos regardless of weather.*" The mission was handed to the 31st Photo Squadron and Captain Merritt Garner and Lts. Al Lanker and Wendell Jackson were selected for the job. Things began to go badly shortly after the trio took off. As they approached the English coastline they learned that cloud covered the Channel area from the ground up to 29,000 ft. Then Captain Garner experienced engine trouble and was forced to

One of the photographs taken by Lt. Cohn at 01.46 hrs on the night of 5/6 June 1944. This picture of roads on the Cotentin Peninsula indicates no German troop movement whatsoever. *(credit: Air Force Museum)*

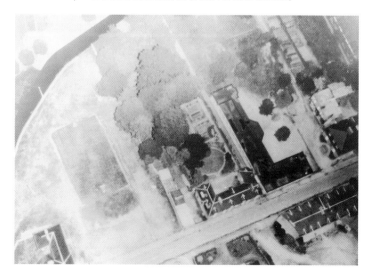

ABOVE: The ground crew and the 33rd PS's Engineering Officer, Captain Donald Frush (second from left) watch as the pilot of their F-5B, s/n 42-68237, begins to start his engines for a mission from Chalgrove in May 1944. (*credit: J. B. Woodson*)

SUPREME HEADQUARTERS
ALLIED EXPEDITIONARY FORCE

Soldiers, Sailors and Airmen of the Allied Expeditionary Force!

You are about to embark upon the Great Crusade, toward which we have striven these many months. The eyes of the world are upon you. The hopes and prayers of liberty-loving people everywhere march with you. In company with our brave Allies and brothers-in-arms on other Fronts, you will bring about the destruction of the German war machine, the elimination of Nazi tyranny over the oppressed peoples of Europe, and security for ourselves in a free world.

Your task will not be an easy one. Your enemy is well trained, well equipped and battle-hardened. He will fight savagely.

But this is the year 1944! Much has happened since the Nazi triumphs of 1940-41. The United Nations have inflicted upon the Germans great defeats, in open battle, man-to-man. Our air offensive has seriously reduced their strength in the air and their capacity to wage war on the ground. Our Home Fronts have given us an overwhelming superiority in weapons and munitions of war, and placed at our disposal great reserves of trained fighting men. The tide has turned! The free men of the world are marching together to Victory!

I have full confidence in your courage, devotion to duty and skill in battle. We will accept nothing less than full Victory!

Good Luck! And let us all beseech the blessing of Almighty God upon this great and noble undertaking.

Dwight D Eisenhower

return to base. In spite of the odds against them Lts. Lanker and Jackson proceeded onward and made an attempt to get under the cloud cover. They were at 1,500 ft when Lanker realized that the clouds were down to the deck and pulled up and headed back to base. He made it home but Lieutenant Jackson was not so lucky and died when his F-5 smashed into a hilltop near Brighton, England. This tragic mission marked the low point in a most frustrating day of operations. The Group had launched a massive effort of 40 missions on this date in support of Eisenhower's attempt to link up the two American beachheads and 19 of them had been aborted by weather.

The bad weather continued throughout 9-19 June and virtually grounded the 10th PRG. On the ground, however, General Omar Bradley's First Army began its attempt to accomplish a link-up of the two American beachheads and to make contact with the British. In quick order the US 29th Infantry Division took Isigny-sur-Mer on 9 June and by 12 June the US 101st Airborne Division captured Carentan. With rapid movement of this type Headquarters, VII Corps had already started looking toward Cherbourg, and on the night of 10/11 June the 423rd NFS sent out four F-3s to photograph road junctions along the west side of the Cherbourg Peninsula. Weather conditions once again plagued the crews and one aircraft was lost during this unsuccessful mission. The F-3 piloted by F/O Kulak was to have photographed the road between St-Lô and Vire. It was last seen heading toward the Channel but it and its crew were never seen or heard from again. The remaining F-3s returned to base with no pictures to complete the total failure of this mission.

The weather finally cleared on 12 June and the 10th PRG launched nearly 60 missions covering vast areas of France. While the pilots carried out the day's missions, Colonel Reed was advised that a major reorganization of reconnaissance groups within the Ninth Air Force would be taking place within the next few days. These changes, Colonel Reed learned, would have a dramatic impact on the 10th PRG's organizational structure and its mission. With the invasion now well under way the 10th Photo Reconnaissance Group would soon be assuming the duty of providing aerial reconnaissance for General George S. Patton's Third Army, and would now be assigned to the XIX Tactical Air Command commanded by Major General O. P. Weyland. As a result of these changes the unit's organizational make-up would also be radically

An F-3A of the 155th NPS in flight. This aircraft is piloted by Lieutenant Cliff Mackie, who flew 22 night photo missions during his tour of duty with the Squadron. (*credit: Cliff Mackie*)

Russell A. Berg, who had served as Executive Officer, 67th TRG, replaced Colonel Bill Reed as Commanding Officer of the 10th Photo Reconnaissance Group. Colonel Reed was reassigned to Headquarters, Ninth Air Force.

The first of the Group's new tactical reconnaissance squadrons arrived at Chalgrove on 27 June. The Mustang-equipped 15th TRS, commanded by Lieutenant Colonel George T. Walker, was an aggressive unit that had been flying combat missions since 26 March 1944. The Squadron claimed the first aerial victory of D-Day when Lieutenant Joe Conklin downed an Fw 190 near Dreux airfield. Later in the day Lts. Clyde B. East and Ernest "Bud" Schonard returned to base from a visual recce with additional claims. Each of them had destroyed an Fw 190, and Schonard claimed a second as a probable. By the time the 15th TRS joined the 10th PRG it had already destroyed seven enemy aircraft and two others as probables. Captain John H. Hoefker was the Squadron's leading scorer at this time with two Bf 109s to his credit.

Prior to its reassignment there had been many rumors within the 15th TRS about it being one of the first units to go to France, and when word came down about the move to Chalgrove instead, it was met with

realigned. What the third Army needed was an organization capable of not only providing day and night photo coverage, but tactical reconnaissance in support of fighter-bombers, artillery, and armored and infantry units as well. In order to prepare for its new mission the 10th traded its 30th and 33rd Photo Squadrons to the 67th Tactical Reconnaissance Group for the 12th and 15th Tactical Reconnaissance Squadrons. The official date of the transfer of squadrons was 13 June 1944, but the actual movement did not occur until later in the month.

Coming right on the heels of the Group's reorganization was a change of command. On 20 June Lieutenant Colonel

After the reorganization of the Ninth Air Force's two reconnaissance groups Lt. Colonel Russell A. Berg took command of the 10th PRG. Here Lt. Colonel Berg and his staff gather for a photograph alongside a 15th TRS F-6C Mustang. From left to right: Major Walters (Exective Officer), Lt. Colonel Berg (Group CO), Major Simpson (Group S-3, Operations), Captain Eisman (S-4, Supply), Major Williams (S-1, Administration), and Lt. Colonel Hibbert (S-2, Intelligence). Note the vertical camera access port in the center of the photograph. (*credit: Joe Conroy*)

The commanding officer of the newly assigned 15th TRS, Major George T. Walker (receiving medal), at a medal ceremony which took place in December 1944. (*credit: Robert Dawson*)

BELOW: The first pilot to score an aerial victory on D-Day was the 15th TRS's Lieutenant Joe Conklin. (credit: Robert Dawson)

ABOVE: Lieutenant Ernest "Bud" Schonard and his crew chief, S/Sgt. Charles Ochs, pose with their *Peachy's Delight* which displays two kill markings. Schonard was a veteran of the unit. He came up through the ranks and was a flying sergeant during the early days of the Second World War, and received his commission as a lieutenant in 1943. (credit: Ernest Schonard)

BELOW: C Flight of the 34th PS. Only the pilots were identified on the original photograph and are, from left to right in rear row: Lts. Keith and York, and Captain Beckley. Note the fake guns in the upper nose of the F-5 Lightning. (credit: Herbert Gardner)

mixed reactions. Fred Trenner noted in his diary: *"Just found out we're not going to France, but to another field near Oxford. This move puts us further away from France and in a newly formed unit. The 67th has begun its move to the beachhead and will work in closer co-ordination with the armies while we shall run deeper strategic reconnaissance."* In a follow-up note on 28 June, Trenner continued: *"Our new field has a pretty nice set up with good runways and Nissen Huts for all of us. Still don't like the idea of being so far from the coast. Stretching gasoline is risky business."*

The first recorded missions flown by the 15th TRS as a member of the 10th Photo Reconnaissance Group took place on 29 June 1944. Five missions were flown, but as a result of bad weather in some areas of the Continent, only two of them were successful. Lieutenant Trenner flew one of the unsuccessful missions of the day, and recorded in his diary a vivid description of flying a recce mission in some of the bad weather encountered over Europe: *"Went to the Brest Peninsula with Bud (Schonard) this morning. Ran into some foul weather and worked myself ragged flying cloud formation. One gets the damnedest feeling inside thick clouds. Vertigo it's called and it makes one think he's doing everything but flying straight and level. In this type of flying the leader concentrates on his instruments while his wingman formates off his airplane. That way a section can keep together whereas if we both flew individually through a thick overcast we might come out of it miles apart. We eventually turned around and came back to base after flying out our ETA and finding no break in the weather."*

The wartime diary written by Lt. Fred "Link" Trenner, extracts of which are quoted in this book, offers an excellent account of the life and experiences of a Second World War recce pilot. In this photograph "Link" is posing with his "little pal" and his aircraft named *Nanki-Poo*. (credit: Fred Trenner)

"Bud" Schonard and his F-6C Mustang *Peachy's Delight*. When Schonard was assigned this aircraft, s/n 43-103360, it was coded 5M◒C. After his departure from the Squadron it was often flown by Captain Howard Nichols as 5M◒T. (credit: Charles Ochs)

In direct contrast to Lieutenant Trenner's mission, Captain John H. Hoefker and his wingman, Lieutenant Joe Waits, encountered excellent flying weather during their visual recce over Bernay, L'Aigle, Belleme, and Alençon. Captain Hoefker recorded the movement of several horse-drawn wagons, and several rail cars sitting without locomotives, perfect targets for the fighter-bombers. As Hoefker and Waits flew their route they were being stalked by a flight of four Bf 109s. The section was about 16 miles south-west when the Bf 109s struck and a dogfight ensued. Captain Hoefker's encounter report noted: *"We were at 4,000 feet when we observed four Me 109s approaching us from the south-west at 4,500 feet. As we climbed for the clouds the Me 109s turned and dived at us from behind and I was attacked from below and to my rear by an enemy aircraft that opened fired at 500 yards. I broke left and we went into a Lufbery. I broke from the Lufbery while I was looking for Waits and was again attacked from the left rear. I pulled up into an Immelmann and dived after another Me 109, and fired three short bursts of a half second each. After the third burst, I saw brownish-white smoke pour from the aircraft's engine, and then he rolled over and went down in a 60-degree dive, exploding as he hit the ground. The pilot did not get out."*

After this enemy aircraft crashed, the other three Bf 109s in his flight turned and fled the scene and Captain Hoefker and his wingman headed back to Chalgrove. With his third kill Hoefker extended his lead as the top-scoring American recce pilot.

On 30 June the 15th PS was the only unit within the 10th PRG to fly. Twelve visual recce missions were flown and seven were successful. One of the sections that flew that day was the team of Bud Schonard and Fred "Link" Trenner. Trenner was leading his first recce mission and recorded the events in his diary: "*Led my first mission today and got quite a kick out of it. After going over the route with our ALO (Army Liaison Officer), and checking on the flak defended areas I would have to pass, I received a few words of advice from Bud and we took off. I was slightly nervous about getting lost over there and bringing back an empty report. Concentrated on navigation down to Beachy Head on the south coast and once over the Channel dropped down to wavetop-level and flew on a compass heading. On reaching the coast of France and checking Le Havre on my left I crossed over and headed down a railroad track. The route I had to follow was of a circular nature and on reaching the start of it I had an easy time pinpointing myself. On a mission of this sort we mark down on our map and kneepad anything of interest that can be spotted on the ground. The contents of rail yards, highway and rail movement, possible supply dumps and anything else of suspicious nature. Then too we can supplement our visual observations with photos. I relied completely on Bud to watch for aircraft and found that time really traveled and that I was enjoying myself immensely. Didn't see anything momentous and on heading north for the coast I passed over Lisieux – God that town was flattened. The only building left unscathed was a very beautiful church. Had some* flak *from Bernay but it was behind me. I wonder if Jerry is going to smarten up and put that stuff in front of us? Got back to base and after being interrogated by Jim Clark (ALO) and Buzz* (Hadden, the 15th TRS S-2), *ate my combat ration and sat around comparing notes with the boys. Hanson and Khare returned, both excited having being jumped by two Me-Bf 109s and knocking down one each.*"

Lts. Henry Hanson and Frank Khare were flying a visual recce in the vicinity of Évreux and noting a large

Damifino?, s/n 42-103131 was coded 5M⊙V. Its known pilots were Clyde East and Charles Read and the crew chief was S/Sgt. Kinniard Allen. Lieutenant Read is seen on the left in this photograph. (*credit: Charles Read*)

number of trains within a marshaling yard when they were bounced by two Bf 109s. The Bf 109s struck from two o'clock but their marksmanship was poor and neither Mustang was hit. After evading the attack the section turned and attacked the enemy fighters. Hanson and Khare selected their respective targets and sent both Bf 109s down trailing heavy smoke. The Bf 109s were last seen entering heavy clouds at 1500 ft, and without actually seeing them crash Hanson and Khare had to settle for probables.

June 1944 had been a very productive month for the 10th Photo Reconnaissance Group. In addition to its extremely valuable coverage of the invasion front and beyond, the Group had successfully inaugurated night photography and could now track German movement and facilities by day and night. The arrival of the 15th Tactical Reconnaissance Squadron further enhanced the Group's capabilities for the work to come. The success of the 423rd Night Fighter Squadron's photo work and the 15th TRS's aggressiveness were also tremendous morale boosters for the Group. Now the 10th PRG could boast that its pilots flew the first mission of D-Day and scored the first aerial victories of D-Day. The 15th TRS was certainly proud of its role in supporting the D-Day invasion and the breakout. The final entry in the Squadron's monthly historical report stated: "*So ended the month. The* Squadron *had made the decidedly unusual record for a recce unit of eight kills, three probables, and one damaged. More important, it had accomplished the primary mission of bringing back valuable information of enemy activity thereby making a significant contribution to the success of the Allied operations in France.*"

Weather continued to be a factor during the early days of July 1944. During the first three days of the month only six sorties, all by the 15th TRS, were flown. On 4

Lieutenant James Warenskjold (pronounced "Vanshaw") is seated on the wing of his *Chump's Chance* (left side)/*Princess Charlotte* (right side) while his ground crew prepares it for another mission. At this point in time the aircraft, s/n 42-103427 was coded 5M⊙AI (A bar). The code was later changed to 5M⊙W. (*credit: Fred Trenner*)

A close-up of the GEE navigational system equipment mounted in the nose of a 155th NPS F-3A. (credit: Air Force Museum)

With the need most urgent but cloud ceilings dangerously low, tactical reconnaissance units received the task of running regular visual and oblique photo reconnaissance. Their mission was to determine the serviceability and repair status of railroad and highway bridges over the Seine and Loire Rivers. So great was the importance of continuous isolation of the battle area by preventing German supplies and reinforcements from crossing these rivers that TAC R flew a number of low-level recce missions in almost prohibitive weather.

Fred Trenner's diary provides a good commentary of the weather conditions faced by the tactical reconnaissance pilots during early July. *"July 4th: Went to Cherbourg with Bud today. We were after some guns that were holding up our troops, but upon arriving there we found the weather packed in tight. Cruised down the beachhead for a while looking it all over and hoping we'd see some Jerries below us. Went back to the peninsula and tried to get in, but no dice. July 6th: First-light mission this morning and it was really beautiful over England. Took off and went through the low gray overcast and headed south. Over the Channel with the sun just starting to rise in the east was a sight I'll never forget. The sky above was shot with color and the clouds below were of a deep purple. It was really gorgeous. On hitting the coast though, I forgot the scenery.*

July four aircraft of the 155th Night Photo Squadron tried to cover the Cherbourg Peninsula at night but weather conditions and continuing problems with the GEE navigation system foiled all but one sortie. When daylight arrived the 33rd PS sent four of its F-5s on tactical reconnaissance sorties over the peninsula. They were to check the front lines and road movement near the front. The 15th TRS also dispatched 11 missions over the area with limited success.

The 33rd PS flight line at Chalgrove. In the foreground is Captain W. S. Scott's F-5E, s/n 43-28584. (credit: J. B. Woodson)

was flown on 2 January by Captain James L. Rose. During February and March the unit participated in the Merton Oblique photo missions (see Appendix 1) along the French coastline, for which the 67th TRG was later awarded the Distinguished Unit Citation. The squadron claimed its first aerial victories on 7 June 1944 when Lts. William Lacey and Jacob Piatt caught three Fw 190s in the landing pattern at a field near Laval and shot down two of them in flames. During the remainder of June and July the Squadron's pilots added 1-0-4 kills to the 12th TRS scoreboard.

The 12th TRS did not remain an "orphan" at Rennes for more than a few hours. Later in the day the 155th Night Photo Squadron arrived, and they were followed by the 15th TRS on 12 August. By 15 August, all of the Group's squadrons were in place at Rennes, and the 10th PRG was now composed of the 12th and 15th Tactical Reconnaissance Squadrons, the 31st and 34th Photo Squadrons, and the 155th Night Photo Squadron. There was also a change of command at this time in the 31st Photo Squadron when Captain Merritt Garner replaced Rudolph Walters as commanding officer, and Lt. Colonel Walters moved to Headquarters, 10th PRG as Executive Officer.

With the entire Group now operating from Rennes its reconnaissance capabilities were greatly increased. For example, during the first 13 days of August its maximum number of successful tactical reconnaissance (visual)

ABOVE: Lieutenant Colonel Woodrow's Mustang coded ZM◉L, s/n 43-12365 at St. Dizier, France. Its name, *The Puff*, referred to Woodrow's slight build; "A strong puff of air would blow him away." (*credit: William Swisher*)

LEFT: Lieutenant Colonel Gordon H. Woodrow, CO of the 12th TRS, and his F-6C *The Puff* at A-9, Rennes, France. (*credit: G. H. Woodrow*)

missions flown in one day was 14. With the arrival of the entire 15th TRS, the total for a single day's missions jumped to 36 on 14 August.

Because the battle front continued to be so fluid during the remainder of August, the month would turn out to be a high point in the operational life of the 10th PRG's tactical reconnaissance squadrons. During the month they flew 432 visual missions as compared to 81 missions flown by the photo squadrons. As mentioned previously, the pace of movement on the ground was so fast that photographs were out of date as quickly as they were taken. Therefore it became the task of the tactical reconnaissance squadrons to search out targets, alert the ground commanders of danger areas, and watch the Third Army's flank along the Loire River.

Not all of the Group's activity was taking place in the air. The rapid movement of Allied ground forces had left pockets of German soldiers in and around the Rennes area. The airfield itself had a triangular runway layout with some woods in the middle, a perfect hiding place for German soldiers who wanted to harass the new owners. Edward L. "Ted" Bishop of the 12th TRS recalled one of

Pilots of the 12th TRS, summer 1944. Front row, from left to right: Lt. Hanson, Lt. Leonard, Lt. Aldridge, Captain Travis, and Lt. Grisham. Back row, from left to right: Lt. Garr, Lt. Brandt, Lt. Kieffer, and Lt. Skenyon. (*credit: Lonnie Grisham*)

spearheads had advanced to within ten miles of Paris. With an assault on Paris seemingly imminent the *Luftwaffe* was becoming a little more active and the number of encounters increased. On 15 August Lieutenant Colonel George T. Walker and his wingman, Lieutenant Manuel Geiger, were on a visual recce in the vicinity of Paris when Walker spotted an Fw 190 climbing toward them from behind. He immediately turned into the enemy fighter to meet its attack, and after a long dogfight with a skilled adversary, Lieutenant Colonel Walker shot it out of the sky. His was not the only victory for the 15th TRS that day as Lieutenant James McCormick, also flying the vicinity of Paris, brought down a Bf 109.

By 15 August 1944 the 10th PRG's photo and night photo squadrons were ready to play their part in the daily operations. Even though the emphasis was being placed on tactical reconnaissance, the photo squadrons were required to carry out a number of important missions. Several missions were flown over the Brest Peninsula to photograph and observe the Ninth Army's efforts to push the retreating Germans into the sea. At the same time the 31st and 34th Photo Squadrons were responding to the Third Army's requests to check for possible river crossing sites along the Seine, Marne, and Meuse Rivers. Additionally, the Third Army was still running into strong points of resistance and needed photographic coverage of these areas.

the incidents at Rennes: "We got there before all the Krauts were gone and on about the second or third day they got into the woods and opened up on our aircraft with automatic weapons. It was a real shock for us and with no automatic weapons of our own we weren't sure what to do. Some of the crew chiefs wanted to jack up the P-51s and fire back with their fifties, but before that became necessary the Army came in and cleaned up."

The situation was also referred to in the diary of the 31st Photo Squadron: "*The situation at the front was very fluid and the advancing armor had left pockets of resistance all around Rennes, with a big pocket at Falaise. This situation kept all members of the squadron on their toes and extra guards were detailed to insure security. Some men in the squadron were instrumental in capturing German soldiers at the base, but most sections were far too busy attempting to figure out what part photo reconnaissance was going to play in this fast moving war to come into personal contact with it.*"

The 15th TRS went back into action on 13 August and launched its first six sorties from Rennes. One outstanding mission flown that day was to St-Malo and Bud Schonard brought back excellent vertical and oblique photos of the fortress there.

By now Patton's armored and infantry units had reached the areas of Dreux and Orleans, and some of his

An aerial view of the 10th PRG's base at A-9, Rennes, France in August 1944. (*credit: Lyon L. Davis*)

ABOVE: Lieutenant Cliff Mackie's F-3A *Sleepy Time Gal*, s/n 43-21728, awaits its next mission from Rennes. (*credit: Walter Campbell*)

RIGHT: The 15th TRS flight line at Rennes. In the foreground is Lt. Frank Khare and F-6C 5M✪Q, s/n 42-103435. On the left side of the nose it was named *Sneaker Seeker* with *You Caun't Miss It* on the right side (the mis-spelling of "*Caun't*" was as applied). Known pilots for this aircraft were Lt. Khare, Lt. Ed Goval, and Lt. Fairfield Goodale. Lt. Goodale was assigned this Mustang during the Spring of 1945 and changed its name from *Sneaker Seeker* to *Mary Margaret*. (*credit: Lyon L. Davis*)

LEFT: Souvenir hunters Lts. James Warenskjold (left) and Richard "Doc" Youll display the German paratroop helmet that they found at Rennes. (*credit: Richard Youll*)

A formation of 34th PS Lightnings led by Lieutenant Bosworth, in F-5E s/n 43-28624 *Margy*, is photographed over France on 10 August 1944. (*credit: Ben Rosen*)

The 155th Night Photo Squadron began its operations from Rennes during the early hours of 15 August, and with the Germans moving primarily at night, its work became increasingly important. On 15 August two F-3As were sent out to check for movement in the Argentan-Falaise pocket. The mission was uneventful, for the most part, but nearly ended in tragedy when "friendly" anti-aircraft fire hit Major Joe Gillespie's aircraft and wounded his navigator.

From left to right: Major Joe Gillespie, CO of the 155th NPS, Lieutenant McLenden, and an unidentified crewman. (*credit: James Williams*)

During the next couple of days the 155th NPS was able to play a very successful role in covering the German retreat from the Argentan-Falaise pocket by providing the ground commanders with some timely photographs, but once the Third Army started advancing rapidly eastward the squadron temporarily lost its effectiveness.

The 17th of August 1944 found the Group's tactical reconnaissance and photo ships in the air. The 15th TRS dispatched 16 missions during the day, one of which was Lieutenant Colonel Walker's trip to the Paris area. As he and his wingman, Lieutenant Bill Boyle, were checking out Villeroche airfield, a flight of enemy aircraft bounced the section. Walker and Boyle immediately headed for the deck and as they outdistanced their pursuers they observed two more enemy aircraft, a Ju 88 and a Ju 52, right in front of them. Lieutenant Boyle caught the Ju 52 just as it entered the base leg of its landing pattern and sent it down in flames. As the Ju 52 was crashing to earth, George Walker hit the Ju 88 with a burst and set its left engine on fire. As he finished his firing run, Lieutenant Boyle fired on and flamed its right engine. Moments later, as the flames spread to the cockpit, the Junkers collided with a tree and crashed.

While Walker and Boyle were engaged in an exciting and victorious mission, Lieutenant Fred Trenner was lamenting his mission to Vierzon and Tours as a dull trip. He noted in his diary: "...*we didn't draw a bit of* flak *or see any movement.*"

A third section of the 15th TRS, comprised of Lts. George Posey and Steve Zondlo, traveled to St. Malo and

Lt. Thomas L. Wood of the 31st PS, killed in action 17 August 1944. (credit: Rufus Woody)

An F-5 of the 31st PS photographed at St. Dizier during the fall of 1944. This Lightning is coded "8V" and its s/n was 42-67563. Note that its coat of synthetic haze paint has faded badly. (credit: William Swisher)

returned with excellent photos of the Citadel that had just surrendered.

The 31st PS's day was not as fortunate. It suffered its third loss to enemy action when Lieutenant Thomas L. Wood's F-5 was shot down in flames. The squadron diary noted the loss of Lieutenant Wood with this entry: *"Lieutenant Wood was a soldier who took a very personal interest in the war as he was at Pearl Harbor on 7 December 1941, and wanted very much to end the war in Europe so he could get a crack at the Japanese."*

One incident of incredibly good luck for the 31st PS occurred during this period. Lieutenant James Matthews was sent out to photograph a strip of a river south-east of Paris, but after taking off in extremely bad weather, he strayed way off course and broke out over Châlons-sur-Marne, 100 miles east of Paris. After observing a river and other checkpoints that 'identified' his target area, Matthews turned on his camera and made his run over the area, and returned to base with some excellent photos. Upon his return however, the plotting section could not plot the photos with the map and reported that Matthews had missed his target. Additional missions were scheduled to be flown to the target area, but they were canceled because the Third Army had already overrun it.

In the meanwhile urgent requests had come down to 10th Group calling for photos of some railroad guns in the Châlons marshaling yards. The 31st made two attempts to get the photos, but heavy cloud cover over the target area

prevented photography. By now XII Corps was demanding the photos and ordered that the mission be completed regardless of weather. While Operations was trying to solicit volunteers to fly the mission, the plotting section called and reported that Lieutenant Matthews had photographed Châlons on his "failed mission." His photos were quickly delivered to Army Headquarters and the guns were duly knocked out of action. Ironically, the mission that had been originally declared a failure turned out to be of tremendous value and resulted in the 10th PRG receiving a Letter of Commendation from General George Patton in which he praised the 10th PRG for its "prompt attention."

By 20 August Patton's columns were driving toward the Seine below Paris and were about to cross the Loing River

Lieutenant Bobby Raymond, sits on the edge of the cockpit of F-6C, *You Name It* for a photograph with his crew chief, S/Sgt. Ed Lamir. This aircraft was coded 5M✪E and its s/n was 42-103229. (credit: Ed Lamir)

Wrecked German vehicles between Falaise and Argentan following an Allied air attack, August 1944.

(a southern tributary of the Seine), but to do so the Third Army needed complete reports on the condition of the bridges along the river. The mission was assigned to Lts. Bobby Raymond and Eugene Balachowski of the 15th TRS.

With Balachowski flying top cover for him, Lieutenant Raymond flew the course of the Loing twice at an altitude of 2,500 ft, a distance of 60 miles, and took obliques from each bank so the shadows would not obscure the same portion of each bridge and so the bridge approaches might be studied. Before heading back to base Lieutenant Raymond also photographed bridges over the canal and made visual observations of the area.

As with Lieutenant Matthews' mission, this mission drew high praise, and a letter from General O.P. Weyland to the 10th PRG stated: "*The spectacular successes achieved by the Third US Army in recent weeks would not have been possible without the prompt and accurate observation and reporting of the enemy's dispositions and movements, which has so efficiently been reported by the 10th Photo Reconnaissance Group.*"

The Third Army had elements across the Seine above and below Paris by 23 August. With XV Corps advancing north-west along the Seine toward Louviers, and the First US Army, British and Canadian troops attacking north and eastward, elements of the Seventh German Army again found themselves becoming encircled. Tactical reconnaissance played a major role in this encirclement. With ground-to-air communications improving rapidly, tactical reconnaissance pilots were frequently able to report the location and movement of German forces directly to the armored columns that were pursuing them.

In spite of poor visibility, clouds and showers on 23 August, the XIX Tactical Air Force was up and hounding the retreating Germans. Fighter-bombers directed by tactical reconnaissance pilots ripped into enemy columns and destroyed 114 motor vehicles, 63 horse-drawn vehicles, and four tanks. Numerous other vehicles were damaged during these devastating attacks.

Seeing the great number of targets on the ground, Lieutenant Fred Trenner decided to join in the strafing: "*(Lieutenant Richard) 'Doc' Youll and I went out today and ran into some excitement for a change. Spotted three trucks going down a highway. Told Doc to keep an eye out for flak and went down after them. Right near an airfield so I took a good look around and then hit for the deck. Lined up on the rear truck and just moved my tracers right up the line. The Krauts had all hit for the ditch and I don't think I got any of them. Passed back over the spot about 15 minutes later and the trucks were still there. Some white smoke curling up, so I guess Jerry will have to walk. Spotted a lone engine puffing up a railroad track later and really splattered the boiler. Gave the driver plenty of time to get out so I'm not worried about clobbering some Frenchman.*"

Next day the weather again limited missions, but the fighter-bombers still managed to rough-up the retreating Germans. Aircraft of the 406th FG destroyed gun positions near Nantes, and about 40 carts of an ammunition convoy near Paris and the 371st FG hit rail traffic between Orleans and Tours. The Fighter Groups' accomplishments prompted Fred Trenner to record in his diary: "*Doc led today and we went down south of the Loire River again. Quite a bit of activity, mostly ambulances. Our troops are fighting in Orleans and Jerry must be holding on the other side of the river. The T-Bolts must have hit there just before us because the road is littered*

Lt. James Warenskjold (pronounced 'Vanshaw') sits on the wing of his *Chump's Chance* (left side)/*Princess Charlotte* (right side) while his ground crew prepares it for another mission. At this point in time, the aircraft, s/n 42-103427, was coded 5M✪AI (Bar). The code was later changed to 5M✪W. (*credit: Fred Trenner*)

A somewhat worn-looking F-6C named *Hun Flusher* seen at St. Dizier during the fall of 1944. Its assigned pilot was Lieutenant Charles "Chuck" Kinyon and its crew chief was S/Sgt. Paul Valentine. Note the code ZM✪Jl (bar). The vertical bar indicates that it was the second aircraft in the squadron coded ZM✪J.
(*credit: William Swisher*)

with burning vehicles. Several buildings are burning. Caught two hospital trains heading south but didn't strafe them. We're quite certain that Jerry is marking some ammo trucks with a Red Cross, but have no real proof. I wouldn't want to strafe any wounded men although I wouldn't put it past the Germans."

On the ground, the Third Army's XII and XX Corps, located south-east of Allied-occupied Paris, continued their rapid thrust toward the east. XV Corps, now operating under the First Army, moved eastward to aid in the entrapment of German troops remaining south of the lower Seine.

The 25 of August turned out to be a day of major accomplishment for the airmen of XIX Tactical Air Force. Its aircraft pounded the Germans heavily, and scored tremendous victories in support of ground troops and in aerial combat. On the ground the Seventh (US) Army was driving up through the Rhône Valley to meet up with George Patton's Third Army, when tactical reconnaissance Mustangs reported large-scale movement of German rail and motor transport north and east below the Loire. The German trains were loaded

with troops and equipment and were attempting to escape into Germany through the Dijon-Besançon gap. A rail-cutting plan was immediately put into place by XIX TAC in order to cut off the escape attempt. Fighter-bombers struck hard at the German retreat and before being diverted to other targets at Brest, the P-47s had destroyed

Paul Valentine, *Hun Flusher's* hard-working crew chief, takes a moment to pose with "his" aircraft.
(*credit: Paul Valentine*)

As the 10th PRG moved into its new base at Châteaudun reminders of the previous occupants were found everywhere, including this He 177 bomber, probably of KG 100, in its damaged hangar. (*credit: Lyon L. Davis*)

266 motor vehicles, four tanks, 44 locomotives, and 164 rail wagons. In addition to the destruction of motor vehicles and trains, numerous facilities such as marshaling yards, ammunition dumps, and airfields were hit and heavily damaged.

After being diverted to Brest, the fighter-bombers turned their attention to shipping and claimed the destruction of two naval vessels and damage to three others. While these attacks were in progress, tactical reconnaissance directed Corps artillery fire against gun positions in Brest and against shipping.

In the air XIX TAC's pilots continued the slaughter by destroying 77 enemy aircraft in aerial combat and another 50 in strafing attacks. In addition to the confirmed kills another 11 enemy aircraft were claimed as probables and 33 more were damaged. Pilots of the 15th TRS were not going to let the fighter pilots claim all of the credit however and chipped in with two aerial victories. The squadron's first kill took place near Paris when Lieutenant John Murtha shot down a Ju 52 that was trying to evacuate German troops from the area. His initial burst set the transport on fire and its pilot crash-landed the burning aircraft in a field. Murtha then came around again and strafed the burning aircraft and many of its escaping passengers were cut down in the hail of bullets.

The squadron's second victory of the day was claimed at about the same time near Betheuil, France. Lts. Bud Schonard and H. H. Hughes were at the half way point of their visual reconnaissance route when Schonard spotted a Bf 109 approaching them. The German must have seen them at the same moment as the Bf 109 immediately broke toward them. After completing a 180-degree turn the Bf 109 then headed for the deck, followed by Schonard and Hughes. Lieutenant Schonard opened fire at 100 yards and saw strikes on the enemy aircraft's wings, fuselage and engine. The stricken Bf 109 burst into flame and trailed smoke it as it tried to climb. As Schonard broke off his attack, Lieutenant Hughes fired on the climbing Bf 109 and saw numerous strikes on its wings. Seconds later the pilot jettisoned his canopy and bailed out.

Fred Trenner made note of the day's victories in his diary entry of 25 August and ended the passage with this significant comment: *"Everyone is now calling us the 15th FIGHTER SQUADRON."*

The activities of 26 August were of an entirely different nature. It was moving day for the squadrons and this move would take them to Châteaudun airfield. Headquarters, 10th PRG had already moved on 24 August and was ready to resume operations from the new base as soon as its squadrons settled in.

The new base did enable tactical reconnaissance to roam over eastern France and even into Germany itself, but it did not solve all of the Group's operations and communications problems. For example, it was necessary for the Mustangs flying artillery adjustment missions to the Brest Peninsula to land at Rennes to refuel on either the outbound or inbound leg of the mission. The missions were long and in some cases, inefficiency was the result.

The 34th PS's F-5E *Snooperman*, s/n 43-28317, photographed as it taxies out for a mission, possibly from Chalgrove. (*credit: Rulon Elsworth via Jim Crow*)

The 10th PRG's next move took them to the former German airfield at St. Dizier. Like Châteaudun, this base was also heavily damaged by Allied air raids, but hard work by the Group's Engineers soon had it operational. (*credit: Lyon L. Davis*)

Third Armies junctioned, and many of the photographs taken south of the Mirecourt-Strausbourg line for the Third Army were turned over to the Seventh Army.

While the photo squadrons were involved in their massive photo projects, the tactical reconnaissance squadrons continued their surveillance of German movements. The Group's aircraft were up in force on 12 September and carried out a variety of tactical and photo missions over France and Germany. The 155th NPS was still flying daylight tactical reconnaissance missions in spite of the losses and damage to its aircraft suffered during the previous few days. The missions of 12 September would be no exception. Lt. Edward Bielinski and his crew were assigned to make a visual reconnaissance of the vicinity of Nancy. After successfully photographing some German encampments along the west bank of the Moselle River and some heavily camouflaged *flak* batteries in that area,

Bielinski began tracking road and canal movements in the vicinity. During this portion of the mission his aircraft was first subjected to intense and accurate *flak* and then it was bounced by two enemy aircraft which severely damaged the tail assembly and the hydraulic system of Bielinski's F-3A. Lt. Bielinski was able to make it back to base, but in the crash-landing that ensued, he and his navigator, Lt. Stanley Stipich were seriously injured.

Lt. Conoly Anderson, flying in the same general area, fared much better. He noted numerous targets for the fighter-bombers. The potential targets included in his report consisted of 50 goods wagons in the marshaling yard at Nancy, ten large barges in the Rhine near Breisach, and a newly repaired railroad bridge across the Rhine. Meanwhile over Metz, Lt. Lloyd Verket was receiving a hot reception from German *flak* batteries. Shortly after recording vehicular movement and a number of goods wagons in the Metz marshaling yards, his ship was heavily damaged by *flak* and for the second time in five days, Lt. Verket had to make an emergency landing back at base.

While the 155th NPS was busy with low altitude missions along the Moselle, the 31st and 34th Photo Squadrons were mapping the Pirmasens area of Germany. Fifteen aircraft participated in this successful mapping mission, but the 31st PS lost an aircraft and its pilot, Lt. Becker, in the process.

The Mustangs of the 12th and 15th TRS, were also in action and met with mixed results during the day. The 15th TRS provided some excellent oblique photos of the Siegfried Line, but had to abort its artillery adjustment

The remain's of Lieutenant Edward Bielinski's *flak*-damaged F-3A after it crash-landed at St. Dizier on 12 September 1944. (*credit: Raymond Gaudette*)

The crew somehow survived the crack-up of 12 September but Lt. Bielinski and Lt. Stipich were both seriously injured in the mishap. From left to right: S/Sgt. E. Budzichowski (gunner), Lt. Stanley Stipich (navigator) and Lt. Edward Bielinski (pilot). (*credit: James Williams*)

Silly Syllogism was the pride and joy of Lieutenant John Kimler of the 12th TRS. (credit: *12th TRS Assn*)

September that numerous detailed reports were based upon them.

For example, one photo interpretation report issued on 14 September consisted of 18 pages, and was later supplemented with 13 additional pages. This immense mass of data concerning the enemy and his defenses was incorporated into defense traces and collated maps, and the first edition was distributed by the Third Army on 24 September.

The missions of 13 September, however, turned out to be the last the Group would fly for nearly a week. It was a frustrating period for the Third Army. A lack of supplies had caused its offensive to grind to a halt, and the weather virtually shut down all aerial activity from 14-20 September. The 15th TRS historian noted this fact in the diary: "*The weather seems to be pro-Nazi, and activity between the 14th and the 20th was limited to a few flights that returned with little more than weather reports.*"

During this lull the Third Army was developing plans for taking the fortress city of Metz, plans which called for oblique and vertical photographs of the fortifications west of the city. Clouds and haze over the Metz fortifications foiled the missions of 20 September, but the weather lifted on the 21st and 22nd and the 15th TRS was able to acquire the needed photos for the Third Army. Lt. Colonel George T. Walker and Major Robert T. Simpson returned to the area on 22 September and directed artillery fire into *flak* positions, destroying two of them. This mission turned out to be the Group's last successful mission for several days. Bad weather returned and virtually grounded the 10th PRG until 27 September.

By the afternoon of 27 September the need for information was so great that both tactical reconnaissance squadrons sent pilots out in the murky weather and lost

missions due to radio communications problems. Lts. John Tillett and Dale Shimon reported the only dogfight of the day. A Bf 109 attempted to interfere with their visual reconnaissance mission, and the German pilot paid for his actions. The section engaged the enemy aircraft and severely damaged it before breaking off and heading back to base with a long report of highway, rail and barge traffic.

Tactical reconnaissance missions of 13 September reported considerable activity behind German lines. Lts. Donald Lynch and Charles Kinyon of the 12th TRS noted many vehicles moving east, in an apparent withdrawal from Saarbrücken and Nancy, and several clusters of German soldiers assembled in fields as if they were awaiting deployment orders. In the 15th TRS's zone of operations Lts. Ted Reger and Earl Ray reported heavy traffic between Mainz and Frankfurt-am-Main. They recorded over 100 barges heading toward Wiesbaden, nine engines with steam up between Bingen and Mainz, and numerous trucks on the highway between Frankfurt and Wiesbaden.

The photo ships were also quite active during the day and continued their photographic coverage of a massive area. Two excellent examples of this work are the missions flown by Captain Merritt Garner and Lt. Rufus Woody of the 31st PS. Garner brought back photos of a strip 10,000 yds wide from Remich to Charmes, and Woody photographed an area that included Echternach, Trier, Beckingen, Saarbrücken, and the Siegfried Line. The photographs provided by the pilots were invaluable to Army planners, and were delivered in such volume during the first two weeks of

The wet fall of 1944 meant trouble for the 10th PRG at St. Dizier. The conditions are evident in this photograph of the 12th TRS flight line. (credit: *12th TRS Assn*)

aircraft and pilots in the process. The 15th TRS dispatched seven missions, one of which was flown by Lts. James Warenskjold and Robert Culbertson. Midway through the mission Lt. Culbertson's instruments failed just as the section was entering 10/10ths cloud cover, and he was forced to turn back. Warenskjold continued the mission alone and crashed into a hillside, apparently a victim of vertigo. In the meantime, Lts. Lonnie Grisham and William Winberry of the 12th TRS were checking on railroads between Rastatt and Freudenstadt when Grisham received a radio message that diverted them to the Dieuze area. When they arrived in the area the section was met by an intense *flak* barrage and Lt. Grisham instructed Winberry to wait for him over friendly territory. As Winberry turned to make his exit, *flak* ripped into his Mustang and badly damaged it. Seeing his wingman in trouble, Grisham broke off from the target run and began escorting Winberry back to base. Luck was with them as the section was able to make it to American-held territory before Winberry's engine seized and he was forced to jump. Within two hours Lt. Winberry was picked up and returned to base in an L-4.

During the closing days of September, fighter-bombers of XIX TAC struck repeatedly at Fort Driant and other Metz fortifications in an attempt to neutralize them before the Third Army began its assault on the city.

Lieutenant Lonnie Grisham of the 12th TRS prepares for a mission from St. Dizier in his Mustang *Baby Juanita*. (*credit: Lonnie Grisham*)

Tactical reconnaissance Mustangs accompanied each attack to photograph the damage and to make visual observations of the target areas. The photographs, however, illustrated that the bombs from the fighter-bombers had had little effect on these fortifications, and it would now be the job of the ground forces to push the entrenched Germans from these positions.

This picture of Lieutenant James Warenskjold's F-6C, with its code now 5M❂W, was taken at St. Dizier in September 1944, shortly before Warenskjold lost his life in it on 27 September 1944. (*credit: Robert Roeschlein via Jim Crow*)

A weather-beaten F-5, s/n 42-67112, of the 34th PS heads out on another mission over German lines. (*credit: Ben Rosen*)

The Metz fortifications were not the only targets for the Group during the last week of September 1944. Tactical and photo reconnaissance aircraft were also roaming over parts of Germany and France, and their pilots detected considerable movement of German equipment on the ground and an increase in *Luftwaffe* activity in the air. Lts. Walters and Hook of the 34th PS reported Me 262s in the Koblenz area. German jets were also observed on the ground in the Schweinfurt area by Lts. Elmer Dieckman and James B. Mowery of the 12th TRS during their very successful mission. This section noted 15 Me 262s and eight transport aircraft at Halle airdrome; heavy rail, highway, and canal traffic in the area and managed to shoot down an enemy aircraft as a bonus. As they passed over Halle airdrome, Dieckman caught an Ar 96 trainer loafing along above the airstrip and promptly shot it down.

The missions of 29 September turned out to be the last of the month for the 10th PRG, and it was a repeat of 27 September in terms of losses. Intense *flak* damaged several of the Group's aircraft during the course of the day. For Lt. Lively of the 34th PS, it was a horrifying experience. While on a bomb damage assessment mission over Germany, he was bracketed by accurate *flak* near Ruschberg and the bursts exploding around him flipped his twin-engine F-5 over on its back and in a dive from 11,000 ft down to

the deck, his Lightning was hit an additional 20 times. Somehow he managed to pull his *flak*-riddled aircraft out of the dive and brought home for a safe landing.

Pilots of the 15th TRS encountered *flak*, enemy aircraft and overly-aggressive "friendly" aircraft during the day and came out on the debit side of the ledger. In an encounter with the *Luftwaffe*, the section of Charles Johnson and Al Frick outmaneuvered its attackers and damaged one of the Bf 109s before leaving the scene.

Mission ahead. Ground crew of the 15th TRS prepare 5M✪B for its next mission. Note this aircraft had two mounting points for an oblique camera. In this photograph the camera technician has positioned the camera behind the pilot, but the secondary port can be seen within the black strip just in front of the code letter B. (*credit: Hal S. Edwards*)

Another of the 15th TRS's sections, however, was not so lucky. Lt. Colonel George Walker and Lt. George Schaeffer were on a visual reconnaissance mission in the Kaiserslautern-Pirmasens area when they were bounced by 12 P-47s and separated. Lt. Colonel Walker made it back unharmed, but George Schaeffer was shot down and killed by gunfire from American pilots. It was a sad end to a productive month.

During the stalemate of September 1944, photo missions again became a priority and 299 were flown in support of the Third Army – more than three times the number that were flown in August. Of these 299 missions, 223 were successful, 61 failed because of weather, and the remaining failures were due to mechanical problems or enemy action. With the photo missions returning to their former significance and operating alongside the Group's tactical reconnaissance, the 10th PRG entered the month of October 1944 as a well-balanced, productive unit, providing the type of support it was designed to undertake.

The weather continued to be a big factor during October and had a negative impact on both ground and aerial operations. The historian of the 15th TRS noted in the Squadron diary: *"The month got off to a dismal start with rain and fog keeping all planes on the ground. Sack time was the order of the day."*

For the 31st PS, which had spent the previous two weeks setting up living quarters and offices at St. Dizier, the rains had now become a serious threat. The 31st diary contained these comments: *"The first week of October the Marne River threatened to wipe out the Thirty-first in one stroke. One morning the men of the Squadron found the river on a rampage with water coming up around the floors of the tents. Personal articles were floating around from tent to tent. Operations were forgotten. With everyone co-operating to the fullest, the Squadron was able to move all sections and living quarters, as well as equipment and planes to high ground, which although not as picturesque an area, was far safer and healthier. The entire Squadron was moved that day and the following morning the old area was under nine feet of the Marne River."*

Lt. "Bunny" Hughes taxies out in his F-6D coded 5M✪Y, s/n 44-14101, for another mission from St. Dizier, October 1944. (*credit: Marvin Renner*)

The miserable weather experienced during the first week of October did not end there, but plagued the 10th PRG during the entire month. In addition to limiting the number of missions flown by the Group, the continuous rains caused the Marne to go on a second rampage. It again flooded a portion of the airfield.

The war on the ground continued to be relatively static in October, with the action marked by limited objective attacks. These probing attacks were basically an attempt to improve the Third Army's positions for its upcoming offensive. As a result of the nearly stagnant ground war, the photo reconnaissance mission continued to rise in importance. Oddly enough, just as it seemed the number of photo requests would increase, the Group lost one of its photo squadrons. On 6 October 1944 the 34th PS was ordered to report to the 363rd TRG, and this left the 31st PS alone to carry out a "back-breaking" workload. Requests for photographs from a number of

The extent of the flooding at St. Dizier can be seen in these two photographs of a wrecked Ju 88 nightfighter parked in the 31st PS area. (*credit: Joseph Gilmore via Jim Crow*)

An F-5, 8V⊘K, of the 31st PS taxies past a partially deflated rubber dummy Mustang at St. Dizier, October 1944. Note the 10th PRG blue and white checkerboard has been applied to the F-5's vertical tail surfaces. (*credit: Marvin Renner*)

bomb damage assessment photographs taken of targets its medium bombers had attacked and placed a high priority on its requests. Secondly, with the anticipation of moving its units into airfields in Germany itself, Ninth Air Force Engineers needed photos of suitable airfield sites, as well as photos of bases being used by the *Luftwaffe*. Additionally, strategic planners were interested in the *Luftwaffe*'s strength and disposition, and requested photo coverage of all German airfields within the 10th PRG's area of operations. Most of this crucial work was assigned to the 31st PS and its pilots, in spite of the terrible weather and increased *flak*, proved themselves equal to the task. The Squadron's historian, obviously quite proud of

sources had piled up at 10th PRG during the period of extremely bad weather. The Third Army, in addition to its requests for front-line coverage, was asking for large-scale photos of fortifications, obstacles, roads, and individual artillery concentrations. The Ninth Air Force needed

what his squadron had accomplished, wrote in the diary: "*Constantly trying to accomplish all requests, it was necessary for the Squadron to do its utmost, whenever the weather would permit, in order to cut down the vast number of targets. One day in October, when the weather broke, the*

Lieutenant Steve Zondlo of the 15th TRS and his F-6C Mustang. This Mustang was transferred to the squadron from the 12th TRS and the name *Phyllis* was a carry-over from its former owners. The aircraft was coded 5M⊘M, s/n 42-103211. (*credit: Raymond Gaudette*)

Finally on 20 October the Third Army received information that a railroad gun was hidden in a shed in Metz, and submitted a request for artillery adjustment. By 16.35 hrs that afternoon Lts. Donald Lynch and Max Burkhalter were over the target. When they arrived at the scene Lt. Lynch tried to make contact with the artillery commander, but found communications were so poor that contact could only be maintained if he remained over the radio car. Lynch had no intention of letting the elusive gun get away and quickly checked the radio contact between his aircraft and his wingman's. Finding it perfect, he directed Lt. Burkhalter to remain over the artillery commander's car and relay his instructions. With everything now in place Lt. Lynch called for the first round and at the same time started a very shallow dive toward the target. With this procedure he could follow the path of the shell and reach the target at approximately the same time. The first round was observed and corrections were relayed to the artillery commander through Lt. Burkhalter, as both pilots dodged *flak*. With Lt. Lynch's corrections the batteries bracketed the target perfectly and the third adjustment was right on target. Seeing this, he ordered "fire for effect" and watched as 70 rounds dropped into target area, starting fires and causing immense explosions. Gathering darkness forced Lynch and Burkhalter to return to their base while the artillerymen were still firing, but later that evening word was received at St. Dizier that the "Phantom Gun" had been destroyed and 22 of its crew killed. For his role in the destruction of the big gun, Lieutenant Don Lynch was awarded the Silver Star.

Bad weather returned on 21 October and prevailed until 29 October, limiting missions flown by the tactical reconnaissance and photo pilots of the 10th PRG. The weather did not totally shut down the 155th NPS though, and it flew successful missions on 25 and 28 October, bringing back excellent photographs of German gun positions near Dillingen.

The weather cleared on 29 October and it was a productive day for all of the Group's squadrons. The 15th TRS, for example, flew 13 missions and achieved excellent results. One of the Squadron's missions was flown by Lieutenant Eugene Balachowski, who located eight locomotives with steam up and a large number of boxcars in the Zweibrücken marshaling yards. After calling in the target to the controller, Balachowski hung around and watched as Thunderbolts of the 406th FG destroyed seven of the locomotives and at least 25 boxcars.

The 155th NPS also returned to the skies on 29 October to photograph targets in France, and lost one of its aircraft and most of its crew. Sadly, it was another case of mis-identification by American anti-aircraft crews. As Lieutenant Gordon Hulse's F-3A passed over American lines near Commercy anti-aircraft fire riddled his aircraft, killing the navigator, Lieutenant William Leavenworth instantly and mortally wounding Lieutenant Hulse. Not knowing if he could get the aircraft safely back to base, Hulse ordered his gunner, Sgt. C. H. Whiteman, to jump. Somehow Lieutenant Hulse managed to fly his *flak*-torn Havoc back to base for a crash-landing, but his wounds were too severe and he died shortly afterward.

The frustrations of weather, problems with the MEW navigation system and now losses at the hands of "friendly" anti-aircraft fire were certainly demoralizing to the 155th NPS, but the unit pressed on. The Squadron, its personnel were reminded, was developing, under the stress of operational missions, procedures that would normally take years of careful experimentation. Secondly, as Patton's Third Army prepared for its next offensive, night photo missions to check on road and rail movement increased in importance. This was due to the fact that the Allied Air Forces had established aerial superiority over the front, and now the Germans could only move at night. To counter the nocturnal movement, continuous monitoring of German traffic was becoming mandatory, and it would be up to the 155th NPS to provide this vital data to the Third Army planners. Progress was being made and the successful missions flown at the end of October indicated the squadron was about to begin to play a greater role in the Group's operations.

Lieutenant Don Lynch, whose outstanding fire direction resulted in the destruction of the "Phantom Gun" poses with his crew chief, S/Sgt. E. E. Scott, and their Mustang *Little Honey*. Legend had it that the aircraft acquired its name from the fact that Lieutenant Lynch was known to be a ladies' man, and with this name he could tell all of his girlfriends that he had named his aircraft for her! Its code was ZM✪Q, s/n 42-103358. (*credit: Donald Lynch*)

LEFT: In this photograph of a banking F-3A the camera port in the rear fuselage and the forward port for the Edgerton Lamp are clearly visible. (*credit: Garry Pape*)

RIGHT: Wreckage of Lieutenant Gordon Hulse's F-3A at St. Dizier after his tragic mission of 29 October 1944. (*credit: James Williams*)

BELOW: *Starize*, s/n 43-21735, of the 155th NPS at St. Dizier, October 1944. Note this F-3A's partial black camouflage on the forward portion of the fuselage. (*credit: William Swisher*)

6

"I DECIDED IT WAS TIME FOR US TO GET OUT OF THERE..."

The Fall offensive: early November to mid-December 1944

During the waning days of October General Eisenhower became encouraged by the steady, although unspectacular, improvement in the movement of supplies to his troops and ordered his field commanders to resume the offensive in early November. The main effort was to be made by the First Army around Aachen, while the Ninth Army made a supporting attack on the left, and the Third Army launched a thrust from the vicinity of Metz. To help prepare the way for Patton's Third Army, the 10th PRG provided a multitude of detailed photographs of the objectives. Included were pictures of each fort in the Metz system and of the terrain in and around Metz. The 10th PRG also provided vertical and oblique photos of the Moselle River crossings. From these photographs the Third Army's Photo Center prepared defense traces and collated maps and placed them in the hands of XX Corps, which had the task of crossing the Moselle. Finally, the photo-mapping of the region between the Moselle and the Rhine Rivers enabled Third Army Engineers to produce an updated map on which new data about German dispositions and movements could be overprinted.

The 10th PRG's work had also enabled the XIX TAC A-2 (Intelligence) Section to prepare detailed data for the aerial attacks that would accompany the upcoming offensive. Photographs taken by its pilots of all enemy installations suitable for aerial bombardment, combined with data obtained by ground forces, provided comprehensive target photographs for use by the strike forces.

Preparations for the offensive were now complete and all that was needed was the word "go" from the weatherman. Threatening weather on the morning of 5 November 1944 postponed the start of the ground offensive, but the afternoon attack on the Metz fortifications by Ninth Air Force bombers was carried out as scheduled. The weather continued to deteriorate during 6-7 November, further delaying the offensive. Third Army planners then met and decided that further delays were unacceptable, and announced that the offensive would begin on 8 November regardless of weather.

When the offensive began during the early hours of that day, German forces were caught completely by surprise by the combined ground and aerial assault. The accurate and devastating artillery fire and the destructive fighter-bomber attacks were a direct result of the thorough reconnaissance work provided by the 10th PRG during the weeks of the stalemate. XII Corps began its attack with a tremendous artillery barrage pinpointed on targets that included 221 artillery positions, 40 command posts, 14 assembly areas, and 12 defiles. The planning by Photo Intelligence for this barrage had been so complete and thorough that not one round of return fire was received from these pinpointed targets.

Aerial attacks by XIX TAC fighter-bombers demolished five troop concentrations, four command posts, and numerous rail and highway vehicles. Probably the most effective of these attacks was the strike against the headquarters of the 17th SS *Panzer Grenadier Division* that served as the mobile reserve in the Metz sector. It left the unit disorganized and ineffective for quite a while.

With the offensive now in progress, a new tactical reconnaissance plan was placed in operation. The new plan, which would be a combination of area and route searches, began on 9 November. Eight areas were laid out that were 20 miles by 60 miles in dimension. Four were covering the Third Army's immediate front and they were to be checked twice daily, weather permitting. The four areas beyond them, each measuring 20 by 30 miles, were to be covered once a day. Five routes were selected and these missions were more strategic in nature since they dealt primarily with rail and highway movement and extended 250 miles beyond the Third Army's front.

The day got off to a bad start for the 15th TRS which had scheduled ten missions. On the first mission of the day, a weather reconnaissance, Captain Glen Staup was killed in a mid-air collision with a P-47 over Pont-à-Mousson, and the next two missions were aborted due to heavy cloud cover over the targeted areas. Later missions during the day were more successful and useful information pertaining to German movements was turned in by these pilots.

The weather turned very ugly from 10-16 November and Group operations were virtually shut down. While the Group stood down, new operational procedures were developed for the second half of November. Daily frontline coverage was canceled on 15 November and a new photo plan combining routes and areas was adopted. Priority was

Lieutenant Charles Johnson of the 15th TRS and *The Sandspur's* crew chief, S/Sgt. Frank Forward, pose with their aircraft. (credit: 15th TRS Assn)

Lieutenant Jackson A. Marshall, 15th TRS poses for a photograph in front of his F-6C, *The Eyes of the World/Nanki-Poo*. (credit: Lyon L. Davis)

smoke made observation difficult over Merzig. Photos taken at Q-1391 small marshaling yard-5 trains, no engines with steam up. Several oil tank cars in trains. L-3101 one train headed east with 5-plus boxcars. Scattered vehicular traffic east and west along highways. Q-3799 one train stationary, headed west with steam up. 5 oil tank cars and several boxcars. Q-2495 entrenchments and tank traps running north and south. L-5012 train headed north-west, makeup undetermined. Q-5996 steam coming from underpass, probably train at marshaling yard at St. Wendell – 1/3 full, three engines with steam up. Q-0875 photos taken of town. Q-3789 enemy vehicles alongside of road stationary, headed north. Q-3369 train moving north with ten-plus boxcars. Q-9669 appears to be a railroad siding or spur. U-9974 convoy of 12-plus trucks, some with trailers in village between Worms and Mainz; 5-plus trains, unable to pinpoint due to weather. No flak *or enemy aircraft encountered."*

The 15th TRS launched 13 missions on 17 November and brought back some aerial victories in addition to detailed accounts of rail and barge traffic along the Rhine River. The section composed of Lts. Dale Goodermote and Charles Johnson was over a German airfield near Kirchkons when four Bf 109s were observed in the landing pattern. Goodermote and Johnson teamed up to blast the first Bf 109 out of the sky. Lieutenant Goodermote then attacked the next Bf 109, scored numerous hits, and claimed it as a probable before breaking off because of a very accurate burst of ground fire. An armor-piercing shell exploded against his gunsight, and wounded him in the hand and chest. It was this point that Goodermote decided was time for Johnson and himeslf *"...to get out of there."*

At about the same time, Lts. Jackson Marshall and Bill Brackett were working over a flight of Ju 87s. Flying in 8/10ths weather with a ceiling of 1,900 ft over Worms, they spotted the first Stuka. Marshall opened fire and Brackett observed numerous strikes before the stricken dive bomber rolled over on its back and went straight down through the overcast. As this Stuka started its fatal dive earthward, Lieutenant Marshall attacked a second Ju 87 and sent it down in an uncontrolled dive. Like a duck in a shooting gallery, another Stuka appeared and Marshall again attacked and fired until he was out of ammunition. Lieutenant Brackett then bounced the wounded Stuka and sent it down trailing a long plume of black smoke. Two more Stukas were spotted but Marshall was out of ammunition and Brackett low, so they decided it was time to head back to St. Dizier.

Tactical reconnaissance missions on 18 November noted heavy German traffic, including 226 trains. The majority of the reported trains were composed of heavy flat cars normally used to transport tanks and other heavy equipment. Along with this increased rail traffic, Lieutenant Ward Kieffer of the 12th TRS reported half-tracks and numerous groups of dug-in troops in the vicinity of Trier. As he checked out the area Lieutenant Kieffer and his wingman, Colonel Russell A. Berg, were met by an usually heavy barrage of *flak,* a good indication

given first to designated areas, then to the main roads and good secondary roads leading to Corps objectives. Pinpoint photography also gave way to strip photography, with frontline commanders requesting many oblique photos for planning river crossings and for artillery firing plots. On 17 November areas covered were increased 20 miles to the north-east and the five routes were reduced to four. The operational changes paid off on 17-18 November in terms of observing German movements and in aerial victories. On 17 November tactical reconnaissance pilots noted more than 300 trains or locomotives to the east and west of the Rhine River, and reported that the majority of the German trains were headed toward the Third Army. One of the more successful missions flown that day was visual reconnaissance of the Metz-Merzig-Sauerlautern area by Lts. Mingo Logothetis and Max Burkhalter of the 12th TRS. Their report highlights the detailed and valuable information provided by tactical reconnaissance pilots and gives the reader a good insight to their work: *"Merzig marshaling yard half full, 7 engines with steam. Haze and*

BELOW: The ground crew of a 155th NPS F-3A checks out its tail-warning device prior to a mission.
(*credit: James Williams*)

that the Germans were up to something and were not happy about uninvited visitors in their sector.

Pilots of the 15th TRS also picked up indications of German movements and reported them to the fighter-bombers. Captain Bob Raymond, for example, photographed 18 targets of opportunity, these including troop concentrations and rail traffic, and Captain John Hoefker turned in a long report and photographs concerning airfields at Kirchkons, Giessen, and Frankfurt-am-Main. Later in the day Captain Clyde East witnessed fighter-bombers destroying many of the twin-engine aircraft Hoefker had noted on the airfield at Frankfurt.

Armed with the photographs and information provided during these two days, Intelligence was able to determine that the Germans were rushing in at least one Panzer

Lieutenant Anderson and crew: from left to right: Lieutenant Nelson B. Huggins (navigator), Lieutenant Conoly Anderson (pilot), and T/Sgt. John R. Palko (gunner). (credit: James Williams)

Division to help shore up the defenses against the Third Army. For its efforts the 10th PRG received numerous Letters of Commendation. Probably the one that gave the greatest satisfaction to the Group was the report written by Captain C. C. Chambliss, the 12th Army Group Ground Liaison Officer, which stated in part: "*TAC R reports received on 17 November concerning German rail movements gave evidence that at least one Panzer Division was moving into the Third Army area.*" It added that the 10th PRG, more than any other group, had been reporting trains and flats by type, and that this had favorably impressed 12th Army Group. Three days later a Third Army G-2 report verified the arrival of new German armor through prisoner-of-war interrogation.

Although tactical reconnaissance grabbed the limelight for its missions of 17 and 18 November, the 31st PS and the 155th NPS had been in action too. On 18 November pilots of the 31st PS flew 20 missions and successfully photographed the areas of Metz, Saarbrücken, Homberg, Sarrebourg, Frankfurt-am-Main, Wiesbaden, Mülheim, Thionville, Trier, Würzburg, and Limburg. Virtually all of the pilots experienced heavy concentrations of *flak* and Lieutenant James Poole managed to evade two Me 262 jets over Darmstadt.

With the onset of winter, night photography was becoming increasingly important due to short European daylight at this time of year. Accordingly, the 155th NPS was assigned more targets than ever before. In addition to flying missions in support of the Third Army, the 155th NPS would also be covering the Aachen-Cologne area for 12th Army Group.

During the evening of 18 November the 155th NPS launched nine sorties, seven of which were aborted due to navigational failure. The other two, however, were quite successful and seemed to breath a little new life into the Squadron. One of the successful missions was flown by Lieutenant C. G. Anderson. He and his crew, Lieutenant N. B. Huggins (navigator), Lieutenant W. C. McClendon (observer), and Pvt. T. G. Nelson (gunner), encountered heavy *flak* throughout the mission, but still managed to bring back excellent photos of the Jülich marshaling yards. The pictures revealed a train consisting of 170 goods wagons in the marshaling yards, and several *flak* positions guarding it.

All squadrons returned to the air on 19 November in order to take advantage of good flying weather while it lasted. The 15th TRS had a very successful day. Its pilots returned with more photos and observations of heavy rail traffic, another aerial victory, and in the case of one section, a good laugh. Two sections were checking on German airfields and had entirely different experiences. As Lieutenant Howard Nichols and Lieutenant Phil Hunt approached the airfield at Lachen-Speyerdorf they noticed some activity and checked it out. As they passed over the field they noted 8-10 twin-engine aircraft in revetments on the north side of the field and a single-engine fighter that was heading down the runway in an attempt to intercept them. Apparently the pilot of the Bf 109 must have looked up and panicked upon sighting the American aircraft. To the amusement of Nichols and Hunt, the Bf 109 slowed its take-off run, did an about-face, and hurriedly taxied back into the safely of its hangar! The opposition at the Giessen airfield was not so timid and the section, consisting of Captain John Hoefker and "Doc" Youll, was bounced by an aggressive Fw 190. The Fw 190 lined up on Captain Hoefker's Mustang, and before "Doc" could finish calling

Captain John H. Hoefker of the 15th TRS added to his scoreboard shortly after his return to the Squadron in October 1944 by downing an Fw 190 on 19 November 1944. (*credit: John H. Hoefker*)

out a warning in his slow western drawl, the German had opened fire. The unfortunate German missed and in an instant Hoefker was on his tail and firing. The Fw 190 burst into flames and its pilot jettisoned his canopy and jumped, but was killed when his parachute failed to open. With his fourth victory Captain Hoefker increased his lead as the Squadron's leading scorer.

The success enjoyed by the tactical reconnaissance pilots on this date was not completely shared by the pilots of the 31st PS. Dense cloud cover over the region aborted 50% of the Squadron's missions. The 155th NPS picked up the slack that evening though, and brought back more evidence of continual German movement and new *flak* positions.

The major story in the area on 19 November 1944 was the news that Patton had completed his pincer movement around Metz. Using information about German positions and troop strength supplied by the 10th PRG, the 10th Regiment of the Fifth Infantry Division

launched a surprise attack at night on 18 November and cut off the last escape route from the city. In doing so, the 10th Regiment cut off a large German column trying to escape and with the help of a tank unit destroyed 100 vehicles and killed over 200 German troops. On 19 November US troops entered Metz and for the first time since AD 451, Fortress Metz had fallen to assault troops.

With the exception of 21 November, weather again curtailed aerial operations from 20-25 November. Twelve tactical reconnaissance, three photo and two night photo missions were flown on 21 November, but achieved poor results because of dense cloud cover over the search areas. The one high point of the day was the destruction of an Fw 190 by Lieutenant John Tillett of the 12th TRS. Tillett and his wingman, Lieutenant Bill Enneis, were on a weather reconnaissance mission north-west of Frankfurt when a flight of six Fw 190s tried to bounce them. Seeing the incoming bandits, Lieutenant Tillett pulled his Mustang into a steep climb to 14,000 ft and then dived to the attack. He chose his target and opened fire at 450 yds, closing to 75 yds. As he broke off his attack Tillett saw several big pieces fall away from the enemy aircraft before it burst into flames. It then rolled over on its back, and plummeted to earth in an uncontrolled dive.

Even with aerial operations curtailed, the Third Army units continued to advance and captured the Metz forts, one after the other. With Patton on the move again, it came as no surprise to the 10th PRG when it received alert orders on 24 November to prepare for a move to a new base. The wait was a short one. On 25 November the ground elements of each squadron headed for the new base at Giraumont to prepare it for operations. Aerial operations from St. Dizier continued on 25 November and the 155th NPS had a particularly successful day. Its aircraft flew strip coverage that evening and noted considerable rail and highway traffic. Some of the Squadron's pilots were asked to watch for German movement in the First Army's area, and as they entered the area the controller warned of

This F-6C was a newly arrived replacement aircraft for the 15th TRS. Note the Group's blue and white checkerboard has already been added to the tail. This aircraft, s/n 44-10896, would soon be wearing the code letters 5M✪O. (*credit: Marvin Renner*)

Surrounded by newly-fallen snow, Lieutenant John "Dusty" Rhodes' F-6D *Virgin!* rests at the 10th PRG's new airfield at Giraumont, France. (*credit: Franklin Pfeiffer*)

Lt. Williams and crew: from left to right: Lt. Smith (navigator), Lt. James Williams (pilot), and Sgt. Lane (gunner). (*credit: James Williams*)

aircraft being downed by "friendly" fire. Prompt firing of the colors of the day by the aircrew stopped the firing long enough for them to clear the area, and then the gunners blazed away again.

The Group's operational flying for the month of November was closed out with the missions of 27 November. For Fred Trenner of the 15th TRS, who had often lamented the fact that he had never had the chance to engage an enemy aircraft, it was an eventful day. He and Frank Khare were on a weather reconnaissance and as they neared Wiesbaden Lieutenant Trenner dropped down to investigate the extent of a cloud bank, and suddenly found himself on the tail of an He 111 bomber. This was the first enemy aircraft he had seen in the air in 76 missions and he did not want to waste the opportunity of scoring his first aerial victory. Trenner took careful aim and fired, but observed no strikes. He then pulled his Mustang up into a chandelle to the right and the bomber turned left into the clouds. As Lieutenant Trenner continued to maneuver for his next attack he felt and saw a powerful explosion; the Heinkel had crashed into the side of a hill, giving him an aerial victory.

During the last few days of November the 10th PRG completed its move to its new base at Giraumont, France. Unlike Châteaudun and St. Dizier, which were established airfields, A-94 was merely a steel-mat runway laid out near a cluster of mining villages. Headquarters, 10th PRG and the 12th TRS set up operations in Giraumont, and the squadrons, less the 155th NPS which remained at St. Dizier, selected other sites in the area as their bases of operations. The 31st PS moved into the town of Jarny, using buildings belonging to an iron mine. The Germans had operated the mine and used Russian POWs for labor. The hastily abandoned POW barracks and other buildings provided plenty of space for the Squadron to house its duty sections and its personnel. While the 31st PS converted the former mining/POW facilities into its new home, the 15th TRS was preparing its new quarters in a 14th-century chateau at Tichemont. The weather was appalling and the continuous rain and ankle-deep mud interfered with the Engineers' attempts

German nightfighters in the vicinity. The crews strained their eyes in search of enemy aircraft but none were seen, and everyone thought they had been given bad information. However, when the photos taken by Lieutenant James Williams' crew were developed, they clearly showed a Bf 109 flying directly under their aircraft. Apparently the German pilots were also having problems with night vision.

The 155th NPS continued operations over the Third and First Army fronts during the evening hours of 26 November and again detected continued and heavy enemy movement by rail and road. During the course of these missions one of the crews endured a unique and horrifying experience as it returned to St. Dizier with its photographs. As it was passing over the First Army's front lines a V-1 flying bomb appeared below them and American anti-aircraft crews opened up on it with everything at their disposal. The "buzz bomb's" course intersected the F-3A's flight path almost at right angles, and nearly resulted in another of the Squadron's

The 155th NPS flight line at St. Dizier. (*credit: James Williams*)

Chateau Tichemont, dating from the 14th Century, became the quarters for the 15th TRS during its stay at Giraumont. (*credit: Lyon L. Davis*)

to finish the runway. The delays did not do much for the morale of 15th TRS personnel either, since they were living in cold, wet tents in the chateau grounds while waiting for the Engineers to finish and move out.

Another new element for many of the 10th PRG's ground personnel was the close proximity to the front line. Security had to be tight since their new base was at the edge of Lorraine Provence, many of whose inhabitants were pro-German. Additionally, the formidable Fort Jean D' Arc, which lay about four miles east of them, had been bypassed by Patton and was still occupied by some aggressive German troops. Each squadron diary mentioned its "combat patrols" (the daily supply details) having to duck pot shots taken at them by German snipers. The 31st PS even managed to capture two wounded Germans during one of its resupply trips.

While the Group was settling into its new base, the ground war was growing in intensity. A more determined German defense was noted as Patton's XX Corps fought its way into the Siegfried Line defenses and found itself on the receiving end of some of the heaviest artillery fire that it had ever experienced. From this, and from the quantity of reinforcements moving into the area, it was evident that the Germans planned to defend the area. Photographs provided by the 10th PRG had clearly illustrated that the Germans were reinforcing their troop strength, and the new units had now been identified as the 130th *Panzer Lehr Division* and the 245th and 256th Infantry Divisions.

To assist the Third Army in its campaign, tactical reconnaissance pilots checked the extent of the flooding along the rivers, the serviceability of the roads and bridges, and the locations of German troop and tank

"Fearless" Fosdick, an F-5 of the 31st PS, and its crew. From left to right: Cpl. F. Thompson and Assistant Crew Chief, Sgt. Bingman, Lieutenant Lemont Dunnum (pilot) and Crew Chief, T/Sgt. D.F. Ross. (*credit: Ann Kojundzich via Jim Crow*)

concentrations. The Germans had also developed a new sound-and-flash suppresser that was making the location of their artillery positions much more difficult to confirm from the ground. As a result, finding and charting German artillery batteries became an urgent matter for tactical reconnaissance.

ZM❂L, formerly Major Woodrow's *The Puff*, returns to Giraumont after a mission over German lines. Note the aircraft is now sporting the Group's blue and white checkerboard on the tail. It has also received a fin strake, which is still in natural metal. (*credit: 12th TRS Assn.*)

Tactical reconnaissance plans were revised on 2 December to provide coverage from Trier to Koblenz to Mannheim to Zweibrücken, and the areas near the battle zone were to be covered three times a day. Additionally four route reconnaissance missions were to be flown twice daily, covering the main rail lines and highways as far north-east as Kassel. On that date tactical reconnaissance aircraft were up in force, and managed to return with numerous examples of German rail and highway movement, in spite of marginal flying weather in the target areas.

On 5 December the weather improved and the tactical reconnaissance pilots were up in force in an attempt to honor requests that had backlogged during the past two days. The improved weather also brought the *Luftwaffe* back into the skies and some of the sections had to fight their way through their assigned routes. One of the encounters involved Lts. Max Burkhalter and Mingo Logothetis of the 12th TRS who were bounced by a quartet of Bf 109s near Limburg. The German leader tried to attack Burkhalter but Logothetis drove him away, and then he continued on to attack the other three Bf 109s. Before having to break off Lieutenant Logothetis damaged two of the enemy aircraft and watched as they hightailed it out of the area. Several other sections managed to evade their attackers and complete the mission without incident. From the Third Army's standpoint, however, the most important mission of the day was the one flown by Lieutenant Howard Nichols of the 15th TRS. Nichols was able to photograph the bridges over the Saar River and brought back a full report of their condition. This data was imperative as the Third Army prepared for its upcoming Rhineland campaign, and the 15th TRS made continued checks on the bridges during the next few days.

The 31st PS was also to play a role in the preparations for the Rhineland campaign. Its assignment was to provide front-line photo coverage to a depth of 15,000 yds behind German lines. Weather delayed these flights until 11 December and when they did begin, some ominous signs were noticed almost immediately. Lieutenant Russell Mykyten flew a successful mission over Saarbrücken on 12 December and met some *flak*, but when Major Merritt Garner and Captain Rufus Woody returned to the area three days later it was a different story. Both pilots received a very "hot" welcome from *flak* and Fw 190s and both missions were disrupted. Other pilots from the 31st PS and the tactical reconnaissance squadrons also reported increased activity by the *Luftwaffe* in addition to extremely heavy road and rail movement on the ground. These indicators should have spelled out to Army Intelligence that something was about to happen. Yet somehow the significance of these reports was missed, and while Allied commanders continued to plan for the drive into Germany, Field Marshal von Rundstedt, the German Commander-in-Chief West, launched his massive offensive in the Ardennes.

ABOVE: A Mustang of the 12th TRS taxies down the rain-drenched runway at Giraumont for its mission of 7 December 1944. (*credit: Robert Dawson*)

BELOW: S/Sgt. Ray Gaudette and a 15th TRS F-6D at Giraumont. This aircraft was coded 5M❂Z, s/n 44-14775. (*credit: Raymond Gaudette*)

7

"WE SHALL NOT BE OUTDONE"
The Battle of the Bulge: mid-December 1944 to January 1945

With the Red Army approaching Germany from the east and the Allied armies breaching the western borders of the *Reich* during the fall and winter of 1944, the German High Command faced the fact that its military forces were on the verge of collapse. Some were already suggesting that peace feelers should be sent to the Allies in the West. Hitler, on the other hand, was adamant that the war could still be won if Germany could drive a wedge between the Allied armies in Europe. Against the advice of his senior military staff, the *Führer* ordered the build-up of troops, munitions and fuel in the Ardennes area in preparation for a grand offensive. He believed that a powerful counterattack could punch through the lightly defended Allied positions in Luxembourg and Belgium and strike toward the Allies main supply port of Antwerp. This major disruption to Allied planning, Hitler believed, would cause the Allies to quarrel and destroy their unified commitment. Then Germany could negotiate separate terms with each faction and accomplishing this, could turn the full weight of its military forces against the Russians.

5M◒M parked in the snow at Giraumont, France in December 1944. Future Ace Lieutenant Leland "Lee" Larson and Lieutenant Henry Lacey, who was to destroy four enemy aircraft, both considered this Mustang as their own! It later carried the name *Nancy* on the left side of the nose. (*credit: Raymond Gaudette*)

It was under the cover of some of the worst flying weather of the winter that three German armies comprising 25 divisions struck on a 70 mile front defended by only six American divisions. The massive offensive caught most Allied forces by surprise and German columns broke through their lines in a number of places. The most notable breakthrough occurred south of St-Vith, Belgium and by nightfall on 17 December elements of the Fifth Panzer Army had entered Luxembourg and headed toward the Meuse River by way of Bastogne, Belgium. In the confusion that ensued Allied commanders were unsure about the location of their own troops, and it became the mission of tactical reconnaissance to pinpoint American troop positions as well as German positions.

Reconnaissance was intensive over the Bulge and was extended to include 12 areas running from Cologne to Mainz to Saarbrücken to Montmédy to north of Charleville to south of Liège and back to Cologne, an area of approximately 10,000 square miles.

The 17th of December 1944 began with a flurry of activity on both sides of the line and all of the 10th PRG's squadrons were involved

When Giraumont was blanketed in heavy snow everyone, including Colonel Berg, grabbed a shovel and tried to clear the runways. The aircraft in the background are the 15th TRS's *Sad Sac* and Colonel E. P. Allen's natural metal Spitfire. (*credit: John F. Miefert*)

in the events of the day. The 10th PRG's two TAC R squadrons put up a maximum effort over the Third Army's front and encountered unusually large and aggressive formations of German fighters. During the morning superior formations of enemy aircraft were successful in disrupting tactical reconnaissance missions over Germany and a number of the TAC R pilots were lucky to escape with their lives. The one bright spot in an otherwise dismal morning for tactical reconnaissance was the mission flown by Lts. Eugene Balachowski and Donald Dowell who successfully directed very destructive artillery fire into German positions.

During the course of the afternoon the *Luftwaffe* continued to fill the skies with aircraft, but this time it suffered a number of losses when it engaged the 10th PRG's tactical reconnaissance pilots. Three separate engagements took place about 14.25 hrs in the Frankfurt-Giessen-Wiesbaden area and seven enemy aircraft were shot down by pilots of the 12th and 15th Tactical Reconnaissance Squadrons. The first kill was scored by Lieutenant Clyde East of the 15th as he and his wingman, Lieutenant Henry Lacey, patrolled along the *autobahn* near Giessen. East spotted a Bf 109 painted in a gaudy orange and white paint scheme flying at 200 ft above the *autobahn* and swiftly attacked. Two bursts from his .50 caliber machine guns ripped into the Bf 109 and it then rolled over, fell to the ground and exploded. The next kills occurred when Lts. Ronald Ricci and Lawrence Leonard of the 12th TRS came upon two He 111s near Wiesbaden. Ricci immediately attacked one of the bombers and scored hits on his first pass. On his second pass a burst from his fifties ripped a large chunk out of the He 111's left wing and the Heinkel crashed into a grove of trees. As the first bomber was headed earthward, Lieutenant Leonard attacked the remaining He 111 and set its right engine on fire. Leonard then came around and attacked from the left side, setting the engine on fire and scoring numerous strikes in the fuselage. At this point the Heinkel headed downward and crashed.

Scoring honors of the day, however, went to Captain John H. Hoefker of the 15th TRS who blasted three German fighters out of the sky and later shared a bomber with his wingman, Lieutenant Charles White. Captain Hoefker was on a route reconnaissance covering the highways in the Frankfurt, Giessen, and Hanau area when two Bf 109s passed under them near Giessen. Hoefker quickly swung his Mustang around and latched onto the tail of one of the Bf 109s. As he fired his first burst from a range of 150 yards down to 75 feet, he observed hits all over the enemy aircraft. The German pilot then jettisoned his canopy but could not jump after his aircraft went into an uncontrolled wingover at 100 ft and crashed. The second Bf 109 then made an unsuccessful attempt to attack Captain Hoefker and then found itself on the receiving end of Hoefker's gunfire. His first burst hit the Bf 109's right wing root and fuselage, and the German tried to escape by making a quick climb to 1,500 ft and diving away. When the Bf 109 leveled out

above the trees Captain Hoefker was right on its tail and finished it off with a two second burst.

After photographing the wreckage of the Bf 109s, Captain Hoefker headed south along the *autobahn* toward Kirch and within a few minutes observed an Fw 190 flying north. Hoefker quickly turned and dived toward the unsuspecting enemy aircraft. His first burst scored strikes all over the Fw 190's wings and fuselage, and its engine began smoking. The enemy aircraft broke right in an attempt to escape but could not evade the blue-nosed Mustang that was following. Captain Hoefker then fired three more short bursts into the Fw 190 and its pilot jumped just as Lieutenant White arrived on the scene and confirmed this kill.

With three victories under his belt Captain Hoefker joined back up with White and continued his route, during which he noted heavy rail, highway, and barge traffic. With the mission now complete the section headed back to Giraumont but soon found another target northeast of Giessen. Here a Ju 188 bomber blundered into their path and Hoefker led the attack. This time, however, the German pilot was alert and took evasive action while his gunners blazed away at the attacking Mustangs. With the return fire being very inaccurate Captain Hoefker slipped in behind the bomber and hosed the right wing and fuselage with his first burst. His second burst set the right engine and wing root ablaze. Lieutenant White then followed up by firing two bursts into the already burning right engine, causing it to explode into flame. The Ju 188 then rolled over and went into a dive, leveling out at 4,000 ft. As it leveled out Captain Hoefker raked it with gunfire and this time the Ju 188 was stricken fatally. The crew of

5M✿A was Captain John H. Hoefker's assigned aircraft. This aircraft was later named *Le Bouchier*. The name, painted in bright red on the left cowl, did not refer to John's skill in downing German aircraft, but instead, to his family's butcher shop back in Covington, Kentucky. Hoefker was shot down in this aircraft on 23 December 1944, but returned to his unit later that day. (credit: John H. Hoefker)

four all made it out of the burning bomber before it headed down and crashed into a house. With these victories Captain Hoefker raised his total to 7.5 and became the USAAF's first reconnaissance Ace in the ETO. This mission, which earned him the Silver Star, was only the beginning of an incredible two-week period for Captain Hoefker, during which he distinguished himself while flying in support of the beleaguered troops at Bastogne (see Appendix 3).

The action of 17 December was not limited to tactical reconnaissance missions. The 31st Photo Squadron and the 155th Night Photo Squadron also played important roles in the events of the day. The 31st was successful in 18 of 19 missions over Germany in spite of the hot reception most of its pilots received in their respective areas of assignment. One pilot, Lieutenant James Butler, drew the attention of *flak* and enemy aircraft near Merhausen and returned to Giraumont with his F-5 nearly shot to pieces.

That evening the 155th dispatched a number of its F-3As to see if they could find and photograph German positions. The need for photos showing the size and direction of German movement was now extremely urgent. Three successful missions were flown by the 155th that evening, and the photos brought back by the crew of Lieutenant Edward Bielinski were of particular note. His crew captured on film several trains pulling hundreds of cars toward the front, and three other trains being loaded in a marshalling yard.

The situation on the ground was becoming bleaker by the hour. Reports filtering back to the 10th PRG indicated that the base was in possible danger and contingency plans for defense and/or possible evacuation of it needed to be drawn up. The Third Army also had to re-evaluate its plans in order to meet the new threat. Patton had already sent his 10th Armored to the VIII Corps on 17 December, and now realized that the Third Army would have to halt its offensive, and turn around to help block the German offensive in the Ardennes.

General Patton's assessment of the grave situation in Luxembourg and Belgium was aided by the excellent reconnaissance mission flown by Captain Edward L. Bishop of the 12th TRS. Bishop, who had been temporarily assigned to the Third Army's headquarters as a reconnaissance officer in early

Though of poor quality, this is a rare photograph of an F-3A from the 155th NPS with the squadron code letters painted on it. This aircraft is O9✪A, s/n unknown. (*credit: Air Force Museum*)

Captain Edward L. Bishop receives the Distinguished Flying Cross from General O. P. Weyland for his mission of 17 December 1944. (*credit: Robert Dawson*)

December, flew a mission over the Luxembourg sector on 17 December and saw American forces fleeing the German onslaught. Of this mission Captain Bishop noted: "The sight of US forces in headlong retreat scared me quite a bit and I turned my Mustang around and headed back to report the situation to General Patton."

When General Eisenhower summoned Patton to his headquarters on 19 December to discuss the situation, George Patton had already prepared his plan of attack. After his presentation Patton was asked how quickly he could attack the German flank, and his reply of "the day after tomorrow" left those in attendance speechless. What he proposed and later accomplished was without parallel in military history. The plan called for the Third Army, which was poised for attack in one direction, to turn around and race 125 miles and launch an attack within 48 hours.

By 20 December some of General Patton's troops were already in the Bastogne area and assisting the 101st Airborne Division to resist a breakthrough. Although the Germans did succeed in surrounding the city on 22 December, they now had to contend with a much larger American force since three corps of the Third Army were now in the area.

The 10th PRG had been quite busy during this period. All four squadrons were in the air on 19 December but heavy cloud cover limited the operations of the 31st

LEFT: A poor-quality, but nevertheless rare photograph of Captain Hoefker watching his crew prepare his F-6C for an important sortie in search of American troops cut-off by the rapid German advance into the "Bulge," in the Ardennes in the winter of 1944/45. (*credit: Robert Dawson*)

RIGHT: Lieutenant Henry Lacey, who shot a Bf 109 off Lt. East's tail on 19 December 1944. Lacey is posing with the aircraft he shared with Lee Larson, 5M✪M, s/n 44-14675.
(*credit: Clyde B. East*)

RIGHT: Lt. Clyde East's F-6D at Giraumont. Here it is seen in the earliest of its evolving personal markings. In this photograph the aircraft is decked out in its blue and white checkered nose band and blue spinner, 15th TRS markings, and the 10th PRG blue and white checkered tail, with two *Swastikas* representing his kills of 7 June and 17 December 1944. On the right in the photograph is S/Sgt. Carl Ward, crew chief of 5M✪K, s/n 44-14306. (*credit: Clyde B. East*)

PS, and only about 50 per cent of the missions were completed. The tactical reconnaissance and the 155th NPS missions, on the other hand, were quite successful and brought back numerous reports. The 15th TRS flew seven missions, all of which were successful. Of special note was the artillery adjustment mission flown by Lieutenant Dale Goodermote, and Captain Hoefker's long, detailed report of German movements in the area. Another of the day's missions nearly cost the squadron one of its most aggressive pilots. Lieutenant Clyde East and his wingman, Lieutenant Henry Lacey, were flying a long route reconnaissance mission. East had already noted four concentrations of trucks and six motor convoys, and was in the process of photographing a V-2 launching site when a Bf 109 slipped in on his tail. The sudden appearance of the Bf 109 did not escape the watchful eyes of Lieutenant Lacey and the unsuspecting German quickly found himself in trouble. The German was apparently oblivious to Lacey's approach and was virtually a sitting duck. Lacey's first burst struck the Bf 109's fuselage and the second burst destroyed the enemy aircraft's engine. Moments later the pilot bailed out of his burning aircraft and made it safely to the ground. After returning to base, a somewhat shaken Clyde East penned this terse remark in his logbook: *"Lieutenant Lacey shot a Me 109 off my tail! TOO CLOSE."*

The day was closed out by the 155th NPS whose crews turned in an excellent night's work. Four of the nine aircraft dispatched found and photographed numerous convoys (rail and road) heading toward the front.

With the Third Army on the move toward the Ardennes Forest, tactical reconnaissance was receiving urgent requests to provide reports of enemy and friendly positions, but terrible weather over the battle area was frustrating its efforts. Captain E. B. "Blackie" Travis and Lieutenant Newman of the 12th TRS made an attempt on 19 December but weather forced them back, and on 20 December the weather was so bad no attempts could be made. By 21 December the need was so critical some single-plane volunteer missions went up to try to locate troop positions. Clyde East, 15th TRS, searched for US troops that had been cut off but had to abort due to the weather. His squadron-mate, Captain John Hoefker, did manage to observe some movement of German troops, but the truly outstanding mission of the day was flown by Captain "Blackie" Travis.

The historian of XIX Tactical Air Command told Captain Travis' story in an official publication entitled, *Reconnaissance in a Tactical Air Command:* "On December 21st some of our troops were cut off and surrounded north-east of Bastogne. Just where the enemy was, and how strong, was not definitely known. It was

Captain E. B. "Blackie" Travis of the 12th TRS and his F-6C *Mazie, Me and Monk*, ZM✪O, s/n 43-12400. The aircraft was named for Travis' wife, himself, and "Monk" Davidson, his crew chief. S/Sgt. Davidson is on the left in this photograph. (*credit: E. B. Travis*)

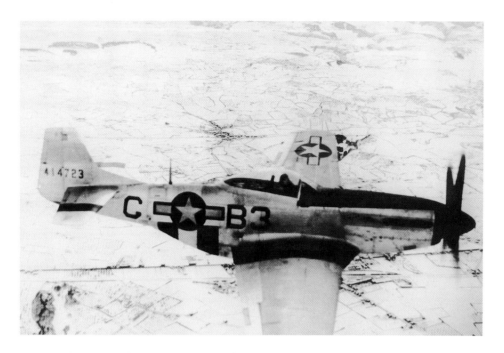

Major "Jack" Poe over the snow-covered battlefields of Belgium in his F-6D, December 1944.
(credit: Edgar A. "Jack" Poe)

air from the east entered the area and cleared away the overcast, and for more than a week good flying weather would prevail. With its weather shield gone, the *Wehrmacht's* movements were easily detected by tactical reconnaissance and its pilots eagerly directed fighter-bombers to a multitude of targets.

During this week-long period of clear weather, numerous German convoys and armored formations were observed and smashed by unrelenting air attacks. In many instances the fighter-bombers were led right to the target by tactical reconnaissance Mustangs, thus increasing the element of surprise and damage to the targets. A very critical area was the Trier-Merzig zone where the right flank of XII Corps was exposed, and George Patton entrusted tactical reconnaissance to cover it for him.

Missions began on 23 December just as soon as the early morning fog began burning away, and the fighter-bombers were up in strength over the Bastogne area. The 15th TRS dispatched six missions to help locate targets for the bombers and nearly lost Captain John Hoefker in the process. As he and his wingman, Lieutenant Charles White,

recce's job to find out, and with the situation becoming critical, Captain Travis took off alone to try to get through to the target area at all cost.

"The weather was about as bad as it could possibly be: Ceiling 50 feet, visibility 100 yards! Captain Travis located the target area and made his first pass, but the overcast was too low. He climbed above it to see if he could find a hole. No such luck, so he then asked the controller for his position and went in on the deck to get the information or bust.

"There were enemy vehicles all over the area as he came in over the treetops, and he was receiving constant fire, but he got the desired information and returned safely home with it. In all he made four attempts, finally getting through to the target on his fourth try." For his efforts Captain Travis was awarded the Silver Star for gallantry in action.

To coincide with the Third Army's arrival in force in the Bastogne area on 22 December, the 10th PRG's previously assigned tactical reconnaissance routes and areas were canceled and their operations shifted to cover the breakthrough area. Additionally, the Group's strength was augmented on 23 December with the arrival of the 160th and 161st Tactical Reconnaissance Squadrons from the 363rd TRG. These two squadrons were led into Giraumont by an old friend, Major Edgar A. "Jack" Poe, former Assistant Operations Officer of the 10th PRG.

The 23rd of December also brought an answer to General George Patton's famous prayer for good weather. A mass of dry, stable

Upon his return from a mission on 22 December 1944, Lt. Cliff Mackie's F-3A, s/n 43-21749, skidded off the ice-covered runway and smashed into a parked P-47. His navigator, Lt. Vernon Red, was mortally injured in the accident and died shortly afterward. Mackie and his gunner, S/Sgt. William McKeon were uninjured. (credit: William T. McKeon)

covered their sector seven orange-tailed P-47s of the 358th FG bounced them and it took some expert flying on their part to convince the Thunderbolt jocks of their error. In doing so, however, they became separated and Captain Hoefker flew into an intense barrage of *flak*. His Mustang took hits in the coolant tank, but Hoefker was able to nurse it back over American lines before his engine seized and he was forced to jump. Unfortunately his ordeal was still not over. Hoefker tried to bail out twice but the slipstream pinned him to the aircraft. Just as he thought he would have to ride it down, he remembered a trick he had heard about while on temporary duty with the RAF. He raised the nose slightly and then jammed the stick forward with both feet and was propelled out of the cockpit as if he had an ejector seat. The parachute opened beautifully but his problems were still not over. Trigger-happy riflemen of the 4th Infantry Division started firing at him as he descended and by some miracle he was not hit. The combination of constant rumors about German troops in US uniforms infiltrating the area and his aircraft nearly crashing into their mess hall made it very hard to convince the GIs that he had not attacked them. Captain Hoefker later related: "What probably finally convinced them that I was an American was the blistering profanity I hurled at them. No German would have known those colloquialisms!"

Lieutenant James Poole, who in his unarmed F-5 Lightning, destroyed an Fw 190 by outmaneuvering the German pilot, who in an attempt to follow, stalled out and crashed. (*credit: Rufus Woody*)

Finally the shooting stopped and Captain Hoefker stepped out from behind his cover of rocks and introduced himself to his "liberators." The next day his 4th Infantry Division hosts delivered him back to Giraumont.

In conjunction with the tactical reconnaissance coverage on 23 December, the 31st PS began photo coverage of the breakthrough area to aid in determining German positions. The demand was so great that its pilots were required to fly two or three missions a day over heavily defended areas at suicidal altitudes in order to supply the needed photos to units on the ground. This monumental task also kept the photo labs and photo interpretation sections working night and day to crank out the needed photos and supporting documents. The *Luftwaffe* was also up in mass that day and succeeded in disrupting some of the photo missions, but the Fw 190s that tangled with Lieutenant James Poole were in for a big surprise. He was on a mission to Euskirchen, Germany

and was at 20,000 ft on his target run when he was attacked by the enemy fighters. Poole immediately pushed his F-5 into a screaming dive to the deck. Three of his attackers soon gave up the chase but the fourth Fw 190 was more aggressive and began to close in on Poole as he leveled out on the deck. As the distance between them grew closer Lieutenant Poole pulled up into a vertical climb and into an Immelmann. The German attempted to follow but did not have the skill to complete the maneuver and spun in and crashed. Upon his arrival at Giraumont an exuberant Jim Poole reported his kill to Captain Bill Hohner, the squadron S-2. An equally proud Bill Hohner sent the following message to 10th PRG: "We shall not be outdone. Chalk up the 31st with one Fw 190 destroyed."

Because of the *Luftwaffe* interference on 23 December, bombers of the Eighth Air Force and RAF Bomber Command struck *Luftwaffe* bases the next day while bombers of the Ninth Air Force targeted bridges and communications centers. These bombing attacks further strained the capabilities of the 31st PS because they now had to provide bomb damage assessment photos of these targets in addition to the frontline coverage required by the Third Army. Nevertheless, the 31st Photo Squadron reorganized its photo interpretation schedules and kept up with the demanding schedules.

Lieutenant A. R. Tenny was flying this aircraft, 5M✪R, s/n 43-12479, at the time he was shot down by flak and killed when his parachute did not open. (*credit: William Swisher*)

Tactical reconnaissance was also in the air on 24 December and flew a number of very successful missions. The 15th TRS flew eight missions, most of which were successful, but suffered the loss of two aircraft and one pilot during the day. Lts. Don Dowell and A. R. Tenny were on a visual reconnaissance over the front when a virtual wall of light *flak* and tracer fire hit both Mustangs at the same time. Tenny called out immediately after being hit that he was going to have to jump. Dowell implored him to stay with the aircraft as long as possible, but Tenny turned west and jumped at 3,000 ft. Dowell never saw a parachute blossom and after circling for five minutes headed south and sounded a "mayday". Seconds after his distress signal Lieutenant Dowell's engine burst into flames and he was forced to jump, landing moments later in the midst of American troops. Tenny was never found and was carried as MIA, later changed to KIA.

Captain Roger Wolcott, who lost his life during his heroic attempt to deliver much needed photographs to beleaguered American troops at Bastogne. (*credit: Rufus Woody*)

101st Airborne Division, which was surrounded at Bastogne, needed photos of the area, and Captain Rufus Woody of the 31st PS volunteered to fly this hazardous mission. What the mission entailed was loading the photos into an empty drop tank and flying in low and slow to drop the photos within the 101st's perimeter. Captain Woody's mission, which was flown through an intense *flak* barrage, was successful but the photographs did not entirely satisfy the needs of the 101st Airborne. After reviewing the prints dropped by Captain Woody, the "Screaming Eagles" made a request for more up-to-the-minute photographs, and so similar missions were laid on for 26 December.

Christmas Day at Giraumont ended with an unexpected visit by a Ju 88. The twin-engine bomber buzzed the field and its crew paid for their folly. John Hoefker of the 15th TRS recalled: "He came over the runway low and slow on his first pass, giving the impression he was lost. The German bomber continued on beyond the base, made a big lazy turn and started back over the base. This time our gunners were ready and lit up the December sky with their tracers. There was no way that the Ju 88 could have made it through that barrage, and after receiving numerous hits, the burning bomber crashed on the base, scattering bodies and wreckage everywhere. I found one of the crew in the middle of the runway and picked up his wallet and identification papers, and kept some of his money as a souvenir."

Two of the 363rd TRG pilots attached to the 12th TRS were much more fortunate during their visual reconnaissance of the Ansbach-Koblenz area. Lts. Norman and Maher were bounced by a very aggressive Fw 190 that made two passes at the section before Lieutenant Norman was able to outmaneuver the enemy aircraft. Lieutenant Norman gained the advantage and fired two bursts into the Fw 190. Apparently the second burst must have killed the pilot because the Focke-Wulf dropped off into a lazy spiral, crashed, and burned.

Missions continued right through Christmas Day and the orders were to fly as many sorties as possible. The

The next morning the 31st PS dispatched 20 sorties to try to obtain the photographs so badly needed by the 101st Airborne and other units. These missions covered areas around Bastogne, Luxembourg, Sedan, and Saarbrücken. Captain Roger Wolcott flew the mission in support of the 101st even though he had completed his tour of duty and obtained excellent vertical photos of the Bastogne area. The films were rushed through the photo labs and when the prints were ready Lieutenant Al Lanker volunteered to fly the drop mission. However, it transpired that Captain Wolcott's efforts had been in vain because Lanker's Lightning was shot down by intense *flak* in the area. Lanker was never seen or heard from again and the photographs were not received at Bastogne. After a two-hour wait for Lanker's return to Giraumont, Captain Wolcott took off with another set of prints and suffered the

Lieutenant Ron Ricci's Mustang warms up for another mission over the "Bulge" in December 1944. (*credit: 12th TRS Assn*)

The snow assisted in highlighting German positions near Bastogne in this vertical photograph taken by Lieutenant John Miefert in December 1944. (*credit: John F. Miefert*)

same fate as Al Lanker. Months later the shattered wreckage of Captain Wolcott's F-5 was found near Bastogne.

The 12th TRS was assigned the task of monitoring German movements in the battle area, but was often distracted by having to fend off attacks by the orange-tailed P-47s of the 358th FG. In one instance, after they had detected numerous trains in the Bingen-Algesheim area, Lts. Mingo Logothetis and John Rhodes had to evade repeated attacks by two of these Thunderbolts. Eventually they eluded the P-47s and made it back to Giraumont with photographs and notes about these potential targets. In addition to this unfortunate encounter, Lieutenant Ron Ricci reported the sighting of a possibly German-flown P-47. He described the suspicious Thunderbolt as painted green with a bright yellow nose and tail sections, with black crosses on the fuselage.

The attacks on tactical reconnaissance Mustangs by the orange-tailed Thunderbolts continued the next day and two of them damaged Lieutenant Don Lynch's Mustang as he and Lieutenant Leon Canady were patrolling in the Bastogne area. Other sections were unmolested by the marauding P-47s and were able to perform their missions. An excellent example of the 12th's successful missions of the day was the report turned in by Lieutenant Max Burkhalter and Captain Bill Winberry. They discovered heavy motor traffic and a possible bivouac area near Bastogne and noted heavy *Luftwaffe* presence over St-Vith.

During the period of 23-31 December 1944, a large share of the battlefield coverage around Bastogne was assigned to the 15th TRS. The squadron carried out its duties so well that it received a Letter of Commendation from General Maxwell D. Taylor, Commanding General of the 101st Airborne, stating in part: "The success of this defense is attributable to the shoulder-to-shoulder cooperation of all units involved. This Division is proud to have shared the battlefield with your command."

A great deal of this help came from missions flown by Captain John H. Hoefker, beginning with his sortie of 23 December. On 26 December he observed a column of 15-plus Panther or Tiger tanks and at least five motor vehicles moving toward a column of American armor. Realizing that time was short, Captain Hoefker began circling over the German tanks in sight of the American column. He then dived and fired his guns at the German formation from an altitude that could be seen by the American tankers. Next Hoefker circled the American column and then returned to the German position until his friends on the ground could deploy into battle formation and go into action. Afterwards, Captain Hoefker reported another eight sightings of German motor vehicles.

On 27 December Captain Hoefker reported two German tanks, 19 locations of enemy vehicles in groups

ZM⊘Q, s/n 42-103731, was assigned to Captain E. L. Bishop. This aircraft has already been retrofitted with a fin strake, as all of the 10th PRG's Mustangs would be by war's end. Note the upper half of the fuselage invasion stripes have been overpainted in olive drab paint and the national insignia has been grayed out. (*credit: Donald Lynch*)

of three to 100, and 12 gun emplacements. No missions were flown on 28 December, but he returned to the battle area on 29 December and pinpointed six dug-in German tanks, three small convoys and a large formation of German vehicles concentrated in the woods. During his mission of 30 December, Captain Hoefker located eight German tanks and 13 groups of German motor vehicles, and rendered a follow-up report on the concentration of enemy vehicles he had reported the previous day.

When Hoefker returned to the front on 31 December, his luck ran out and he had to jump for the second time in eight days. He was over German lines looking for a hole in the 10/10ths overcast when his Mustang was hit by flak and burst into flames which quickly enveloped the cockpit area. Hoefker again utilized the "ejector technique" of getting out of his aircraft, but this time he was propelled out with such force that he lost his flying boots. He came down in German-held territory near Bastogne and quickly scrambled into some nearby woods. After concealing himself in the woods, Hoefker wrapped his freezing feet in material torn from his parachute and used the remainder for camouflage and warmth. During the next two days he moved cautiously through the woods toward American lines and somehow avoided German

patrols that were looking for him. Some of the patrols came within 15 ft of him, but he was never spotted. On the morning of 2 January 1945, a heavy ground fog covered the Bastogne area, which enabled Captain Hoefker to reach American lines. He was quickly returned to his unit and hospitalized with frostbitten feet.

The need for round-the-clock intelligence reports was helping to make December 1944 the busiest month in the 155th Night Photo Squadron's history. During the month the squadron flew 99 missions and drew high praise from Generals Hoyt Vandenberg and O. P. Weyland for its work on 24 and 25 December. In his letter General Vandenberg stated: "I would like to commend the efforts which the 155th Night Photo Squadron has made since 14 December, and with particular reference to the very fine performance on Christmas Eve. The intelligence derived has been of exceptional value in this very critical phase of our operations. Their operations of 24/25 December, without doubt, comprise the most outstanding performance of night photography done anywhere at any time. My congratulations and may we have more."

The photographs of the marshaling yards at St. Vith taken by Lts. Porter and Meltzer on 23 December had shown a large concentration of railroad cars and

This extremely clear shot of the roads and rail lines in and around St-Vith were photographed by Lieutenant Loomis' crew at 21.45 hrs on 24 December 1944 from an altitude of 8,000 ft using M-46 flash bombs for illumination. (*credit: James Williams*)

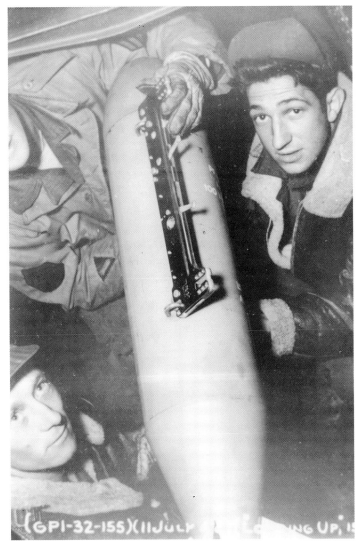

ABOVE: Ground crew load an M-46 flash bomb into a 155th NPS F-3A. (*credit: James Williams*)

BELOW: Captain Bob Dawson runs up the engine of 5M❂R in preparation for his mission over the "Bulge," December 1944. (*credit: Robert Dawson*)

locomotives, and placed this target high on the priority list. The next day three squadrons of US bombers hit the marshaling yards, and the RAF followed up with another strike at night. On Christmas Eve the 155th NPS was up again and some of its crews met with strong opposition from *flak* and night fighters. This was especially true for Lts. Camp and Kezziah whose F-3A was hit at least 45 times by guns from German night fighters, and both men received wounds. Other crews were luckier. Lts. Loomis and Reeves were able to bring back clear photographs illustrating the destruction of the roads and railroads leading into St-Vith.

On Christmas night the 155th NPS successfully completed 13 of 17 missions in spite of harassment by German night fighters. The F-3A piloted by Lieutenant Bielinski became the prey of two or more Me 410s, which in turn were being pursued by two P-61 Black Widows. Probably what broke the "stalemate" was the insistent cries of the radar controller who kept shouting at Bielinski: "Can't you go any faster?" Hearing these pleas, Lieutenant Bielinski pushed his throttles all the way forward and made a "record shattering" dash back to base and safety!

The 155th NPS's successful missions continued throughout the month in spite of strong night fighter opposition, *flak*, and Allied guns. A near-fatal incident took place on 29 December when two of the squadron's F-3As were attacked by P-61s. The Havoc flown by Lieutenant Jim Williams was hit several times before the Black Widow pilots realized their error and broke off the attack. Fortunately Williams was able to return safely to the base. On the following night Lieutenant Bielinski was approaching the field for a landing when his aircraft was subjected to fire from about every "friendly" battery surrounding the field. Somehow his aircraft made it through the storm of *flak* and landed safely. This incident was the last straw for Major Joe Gillespie, CO of the 155th NPS. He angrily demanded that better recognition systems be devised by XIX TAC, and reminded everyone of the problem with the caustic remark: "Day flyers are killed in combat, it is said. Night flyers kill themselves. There is certainly no reason for our friends to aid in the destruction!"

As 1944 drew to a close, the situation on the ground stabilized as a result of the battering given to the Germans by the combined efforts of American air and ground forces. During the last four days of the year fierce fighting took place along the entire Third Army front. Losses were heavy but George Patton's troops blunted the assault. The most ferocious fighting took place on 31 December when the Germans

Lt. Eugene Balachowski's *Dottie* parked on its snow-covered hard stand at Giraumont, December 1944. Wartime sensors have cut the "5M" code out of this photograph. (*credit: Eugene Balachowski*)

launched 17 attacks, supported by 64 raids by the *Luftwaffe*, against the Third Army. Even though it again suffered heavy casualties, the Third Army stood firm and not only repulsed the attack, but made a few small advances as well. In order to celebrate the victory and welcome in the New Year, Patton ordered a spectacular "greeting" to his adversaries: a 20-minute rapid fire barrage by every battery under his command into their positions.

During the early morning hours of 1 January 1945, the *Luftwaffe* launched a major air attack, codenamed Operation *Bodenplatte*, against 16 Allied airfields located in the Low Countries and north-eastern France. The Germans believed that the destruction of these bases would end Allied air superiority, and allow their fighters to more effectively defend their cities against Allied bombing raids. The attack did succeed in destroying about 200 Allied aircraft, but at a cost the *Luftwaffe* could not afford. After this failure the German High Command realized that its Ardennes offensive was doomed and went on the defensive in the "Bulge" area. Then, under the cover of deteriorating weather, the Germans began an organized withdrawal. While some forces withdrew under the cover of the harsh weather that had severely hampered Allied aerial operations, the remaining German elements engaged the Allies. Along with a holding action on the Bastogne front, the Germans also launched a diversionary offensive in the Strasbourg area in order to draw

Captain Robert Holbury who flew the vital and extremely dangerous mission along the Saar and Moselle Rivers on 1 January 1945.
(*credit: Rufus Woody*)

Allied air and ground forces away from the "Bulge". The thrust into the Alsatian Plain was first noted when aerial reconnaissance detected roadbed coverings on barges along the Saar River between Merzig and the Moselle River to the north. Reconnaissance aircraft also reported that bridge ends were under construction at several points. Allied Intelligence was convinced that the barges could be quickly moved into place at these bridge ends to provide an avenue for Panzer units located nearby to launch an attack into this thinly held sector. With the weather worsening it was of paramount importance to obtain photos of German movements, and with a ceiling of only 600 ft that day a "dicing" mission was the only way to accomplish the mission.

The mission request arrived at 10th PRG on a day that all other missions had been scrubbed due to the weather. With these conditions in mind Captain Robert Holbury, assistant Group Operations Officer, volunteered to fly it himself rather than assign such a hazardous mission to another pilot.

Taking off in F-5 Lightning No. 608, Captain Holbury headed directly toward the heavily defended 12-mile sector and began his camera run at Merzig, north along the Saar to the Moselle, then made a left turn down the Moselle to complete the mission. Holbury recalled: "It occupied my full attention to follow the river and at the same time avoid hitting obstacles. Hills were above me on either side most of the way and I concentrated on staying as low as possible. Jerries were firing at me, but I was too busy to do anything but follow the river. Suddenly red balls, about three-quarters the size of billiard balls, were arching around me. I felt several sharp impacts as the wheel tried to jerk out of my hands and the right rudder pedal went forward. It took heavy pressure to neutralize the controls, but they responded normally.

"I flew as close to the ground as possible while I looked for the damage. My left coolant gauge was creeping past the red line. A glance in the rear-view mirror showed a stream of white vapor behind me. I immediately feathered the prop. By this time I didn't know where I was – all my careful memorizing of the route was forgotten.

ABOVE: This F-6C was one of the most well-known Mustangs in the 15th TRS. It was Captain John Hoefker's favorite aircraft and in it he scored his first three aerial victories. Note the kill markings and mission markers are in red. Standing on the wing in this photograph is Lieutenant Colonel Bob Simpson. *(credit: Ralph Woolner via Jeff Ethell)*

BELOW: A beautiful shot of the 34th PS's F-5E *Strato Snob* at Chalgrove, summer 1944. The pilot of s/n 44-23235 was Lieutenant Schmidt. *(credit: Richard Kill)*

ABOVE: The 34th PS's F-5E *Ma Petite Cherie II*, s/n 44-28329 at Chalgrove. The pilot of this aircraft was Captain Ray Beckley. *(credit: Richard Kill)*

BELOW: Lt. Stanley Newman's F-6C *'Azel* at Furth, Germany. Its codes were IX✪H, s/n 42-103213. The aircraft bore the name *Boomerang* on the right side of the nose. *(credit: Stanley Newman)*

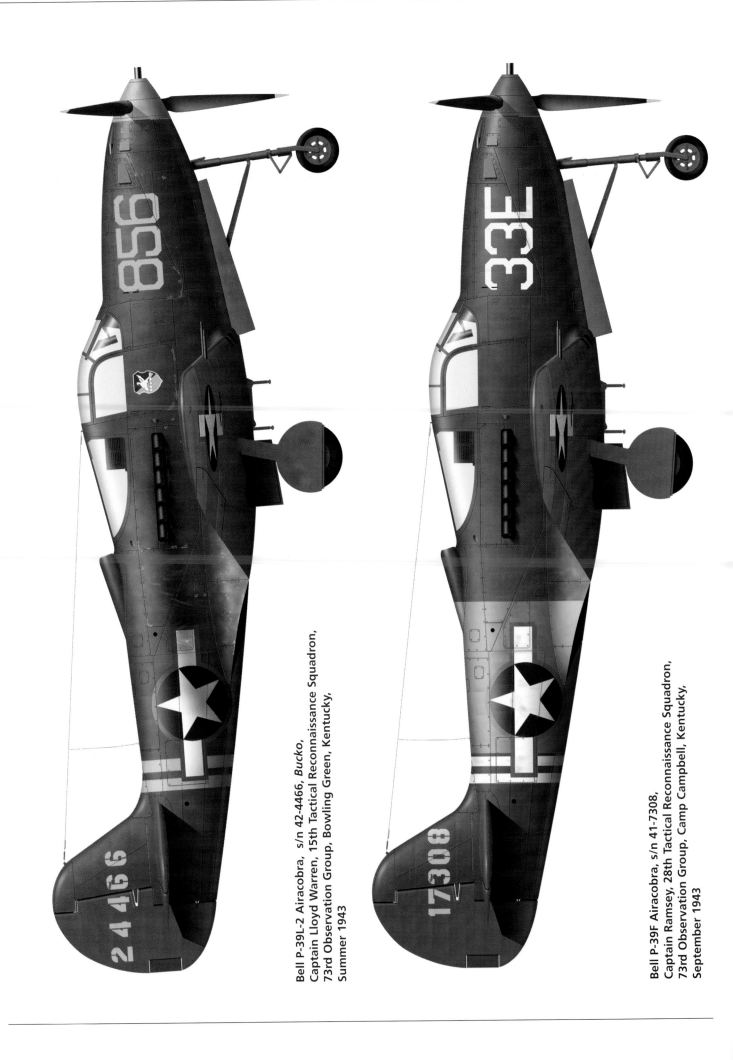

Bell P-39L-2 Airacobra, s/n 42-4466, *Bucko*,
Captain Lloyd Warren, 15th Tactical Reconnaissance Squadron,
73rd Observation Group, Bowling Green, Kentucky,
Summer 1943

Bell P-39F Airacobra, s/n 41-7308,
Captain Ramsey, 28th Tactical Reconnaissance Squadron,
73rd Observation Group, Camp Campbell, Kentucky,
September 1943

Curtis P-40N Warhawk, s/n 42-105596,
Commanding Officer, 152nd Tactical Reconnaissance Squadron,
73rd Observation Group, Camp Campbell, Kentucky,
September 1943

Bell P-39N Airacobra, s/n 42-18899,
152nd Tactical Reconnaissance Squadron,
73rd Observation Group, Berry Field, Tennessee,
September 1943

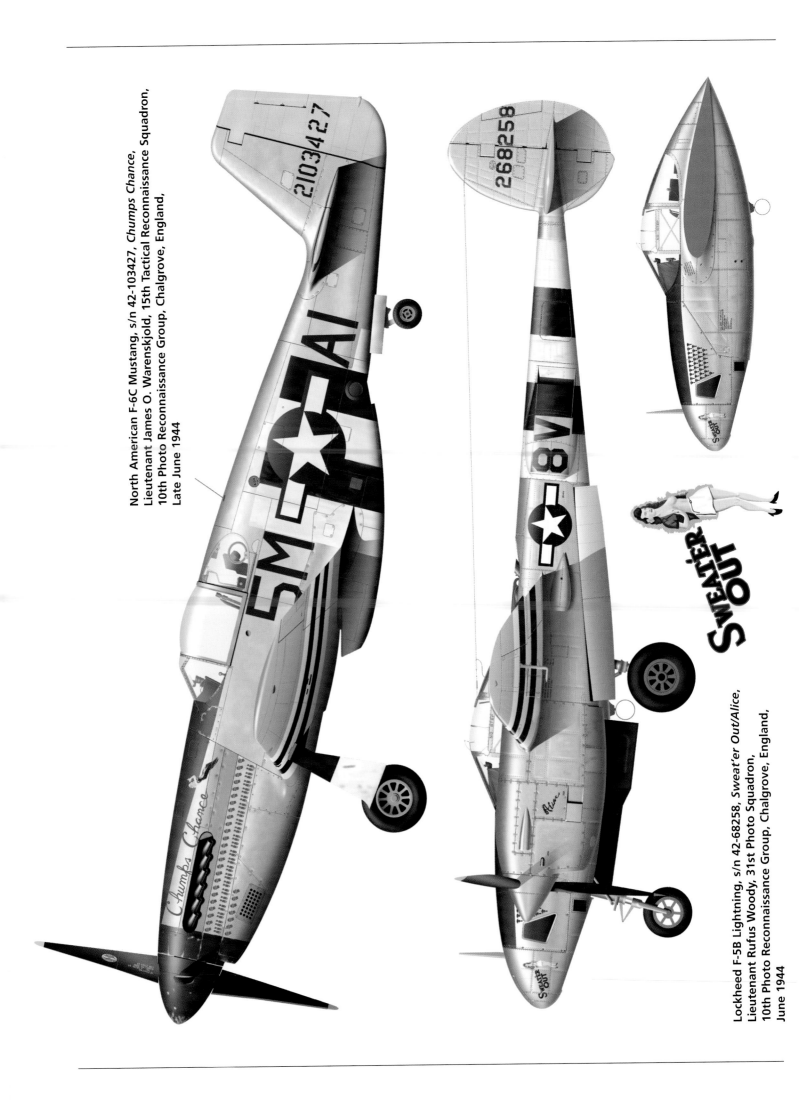

North American F-6C Mustang, s/n 42-103427, *Chumps Chance*,
Lieutenant James O. Warenskjold, 15th Tactical Reconnaissance Squadron,
10th Photo Reconnaissance Group, Chalgrove, England,
Late June 1944

Lockheed F-5B Lightning, s/n 42-68258, *Sweat'er Out/Alice*,
Lieutenant Rufus Woody, 31st Photo Squadron,
10th Photo Reconnaissance Group, Chalgrove, England,
June 1944

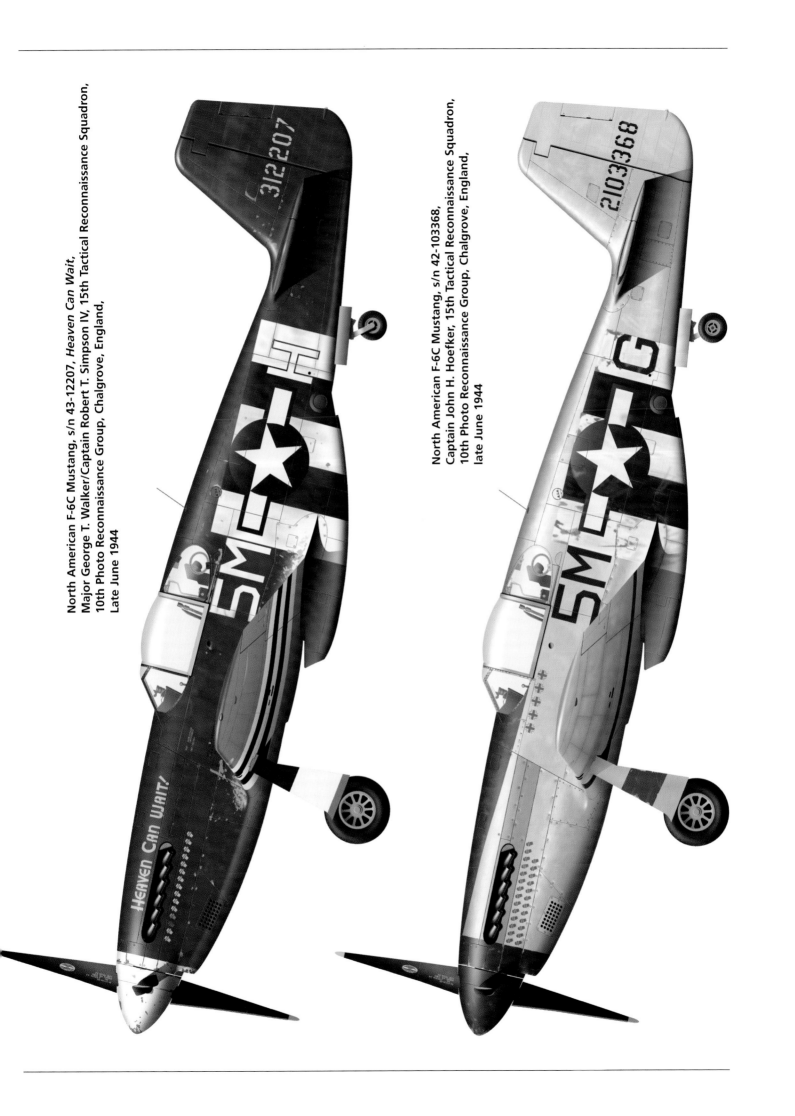

North American F-6C Mustang, s/n 43-12207, *Heaven Can Wait*,
Major George T. Walker/Captain Robert T. Simpson IV, 15th Tactical Reconnaissance Squadron,
10th Photo Reconnaissance Group, Chalgrove, England,
Late June 1944

North American F-6C Mustang, s/n 42-103368,
Captain John H. Hoefker, 15th Tactical Reconnaissance Squadron,
10th Photo Reconnaissance Group, Chalgrove, England,
late June 1944

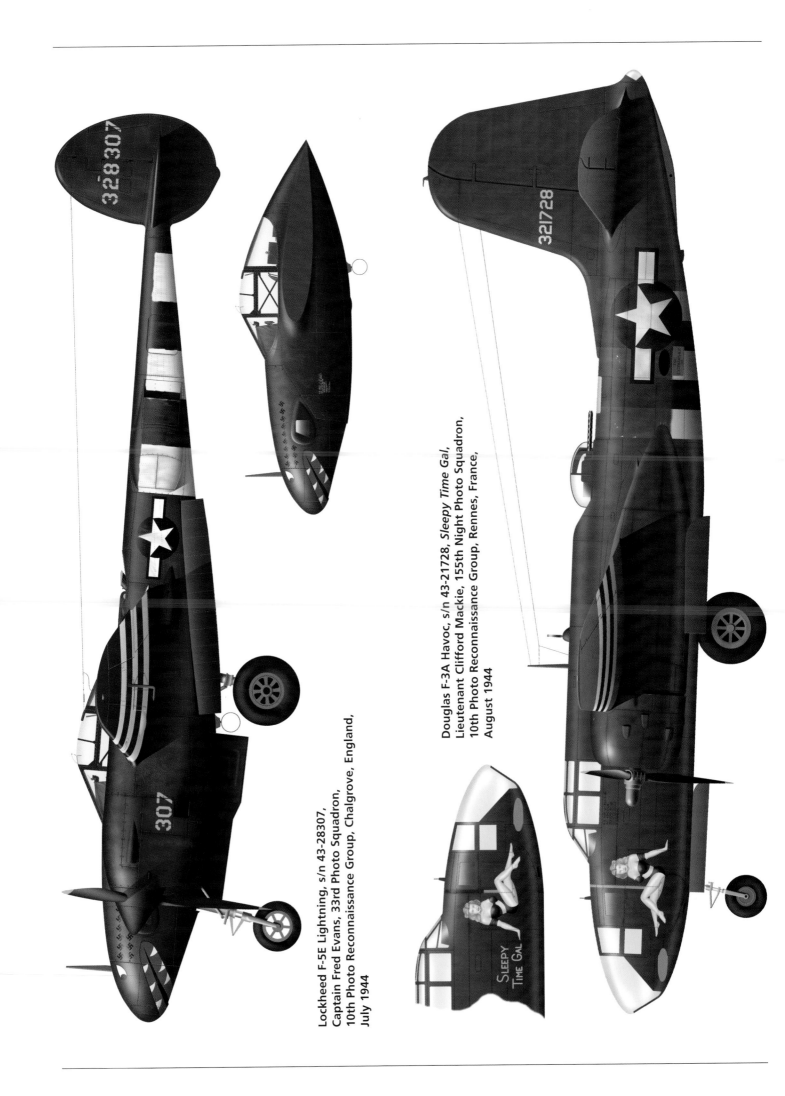

Lockheed F-5E Lightning, s/n 43-28307,
Captain Fred Evans, 33rd Photo Squadron,
10th Photo Reconnaissance Group, Chalgrove, England,
July 1944

Douglas F-3A Havoc, s/n 43-21728, *Sleepy Time Gal*,
Lieutenant Clifford Mackie, 155th Night Photo Squadron,
10th Photo Reconnaissance Group, Rennes, France,
August 1944

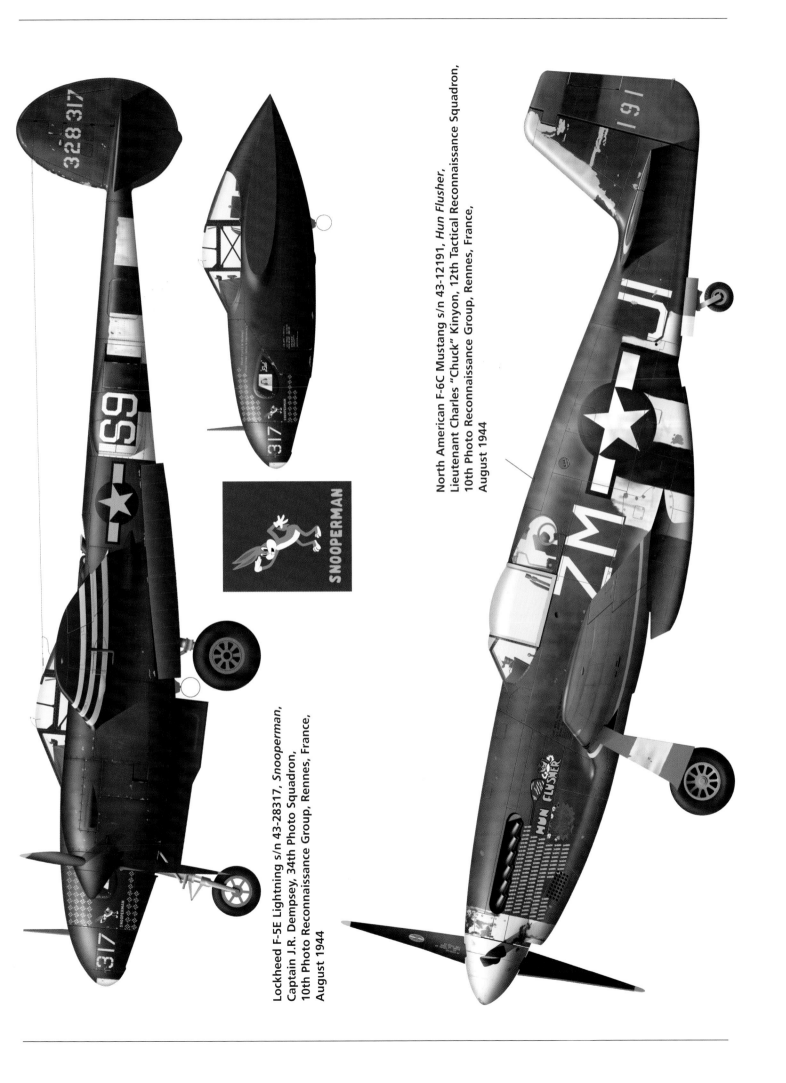

Lockheed F-5E Lightning s/n 43-28317, *Snooperman*,
Captain J.R. Dempsey, 34th Photo Squadron,
10th Photo Reconnaissance Group, Rennes, France,
August 1944

North American F-6C Mustang s/n 43-12191, *Hun Flusher*,
Lieutenant Charles "Chuck" Kinyon, 12th Tactical Reconnaissance Squadron,
10th Photo Reconnaissance Group, Rennes, France,
August 1944

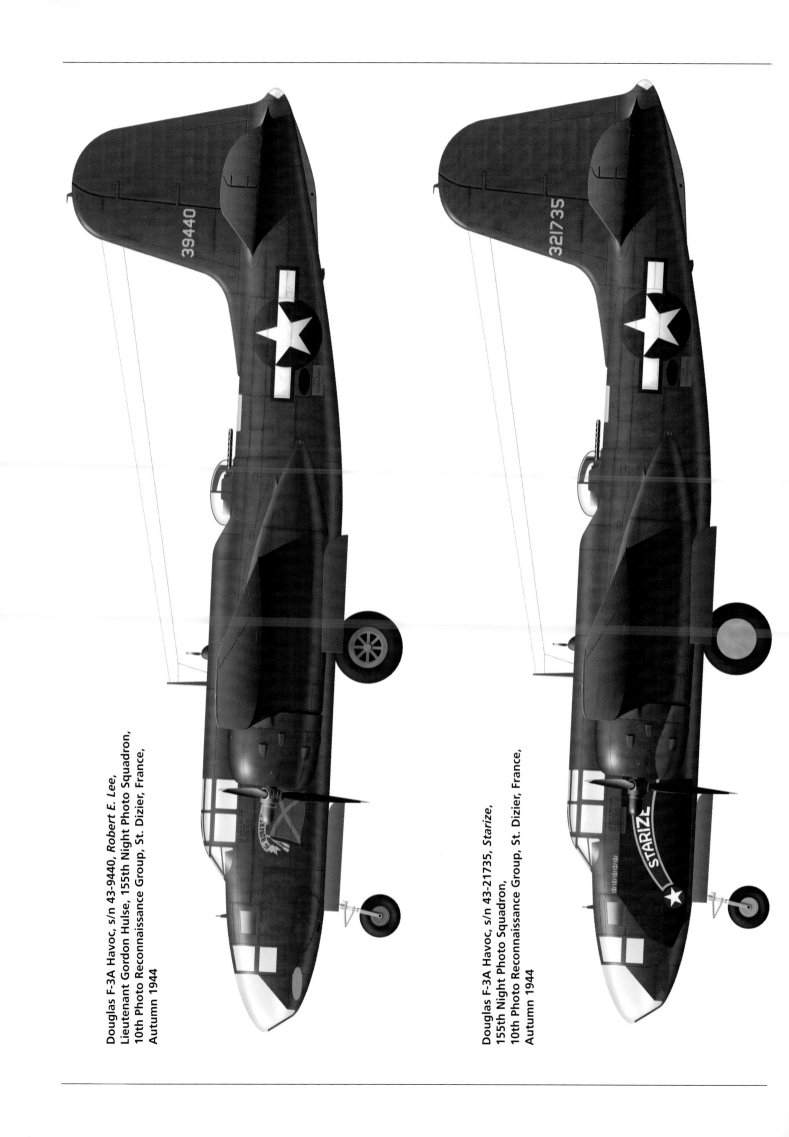

Douglas F-3A Havoc, s/n 43-9440, *Robert E. Lee*,
Lieutenant Gordon Hulse, 155th Night Photo Squadron,
10th Photo Reconnaissance Group, St. Dizier, France,
Autumn 1944

Douglas F-3A Havoc, s/n 43-21735, *Starize*,
155th Night Photo Squadron,
10th Photo Reconnaissance Group, St. Dizier, France,
Autumn 1944

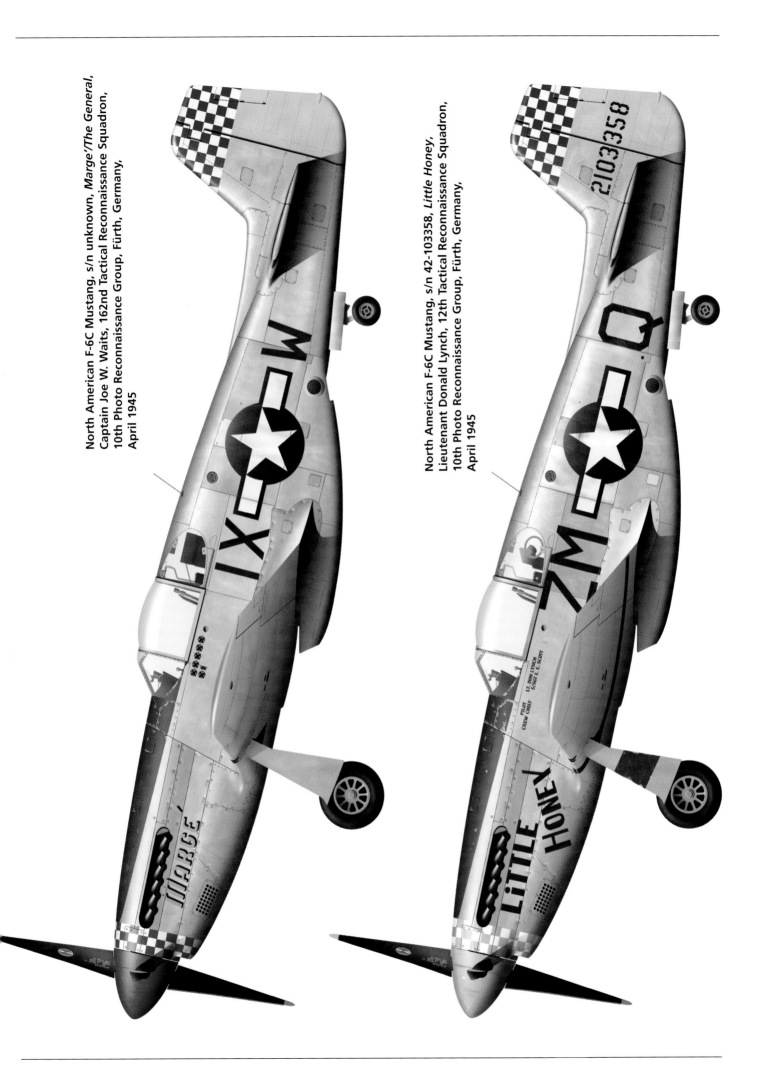

North American F-6C Mustang, s/n unknown, *Marge*/*The General*, Captain Joe W. Waits, 162nd Tactical Reconnaissance Squadron, 10th Photo Reconnaissance Group, Fürth, Germany, April 1945

North American F-6C Mustang, s/n 42-103358, *Little Honey*, Lieutenant Donald Lynch, 12th Tactical Reconnaissance Squadron, 10th Photo Reconnaissance Group, Fürth, Germany, April 1945

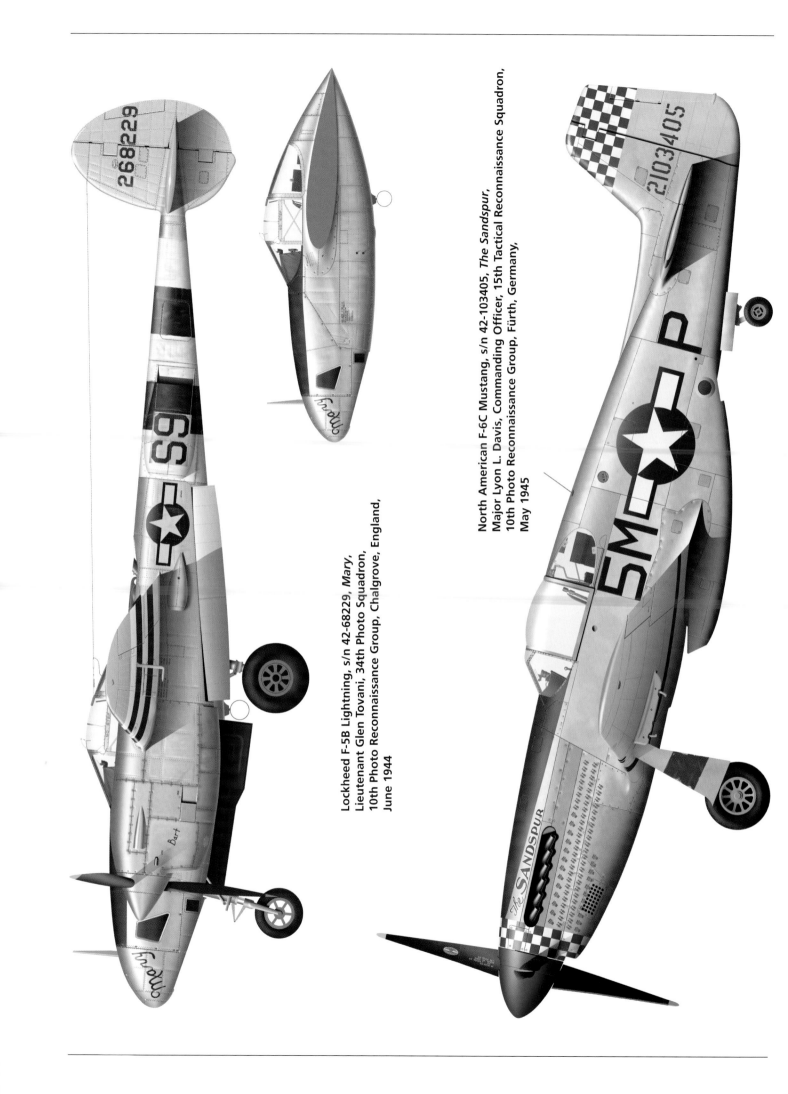

Lockheed F-5B Lightning, s/n 42-68229, *Mary*,
Lieutenant Glen Tovani, 34th Photo Squadron,
10th Photo Reconnaissance Group, Chalgrove, England,
June 1944

North American F-6C Mustang, s/n 42-103405, *The Sandspur*,
Major Lyon L. Davis, Commanding Officer, 15th Tactical Reconnaissance Squadron,
10th Photo Reconnaissance Group, Fürth, Germany,
May 1945

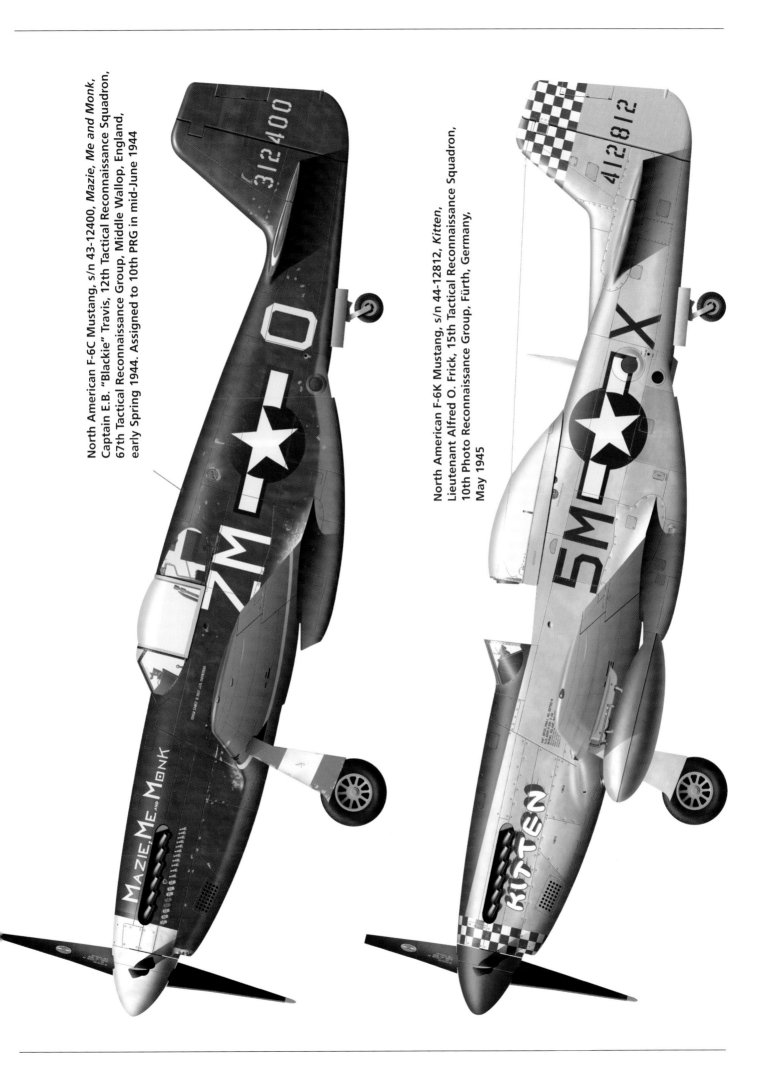

North American F-6C Mustang, s/n 43-12400, *Mazie, Me and Monk*, Captain E.B. "Blackie" Travis, 12th Tactical Reconnaissance Squadron, 67th Tactical Reconnaissance Group, Middle Wallop, England, early Spring 1944. Assigned to 10th PRG in mid-June 1944

North American F-6K Mustang, s/n 44-12812, *Kitten*, Lieutenant Alfred O. Frick, 15th Tactical Reconnaissance Squadron, 10th Photo Reconnaissance Group, Fürth, Germany, May 1945

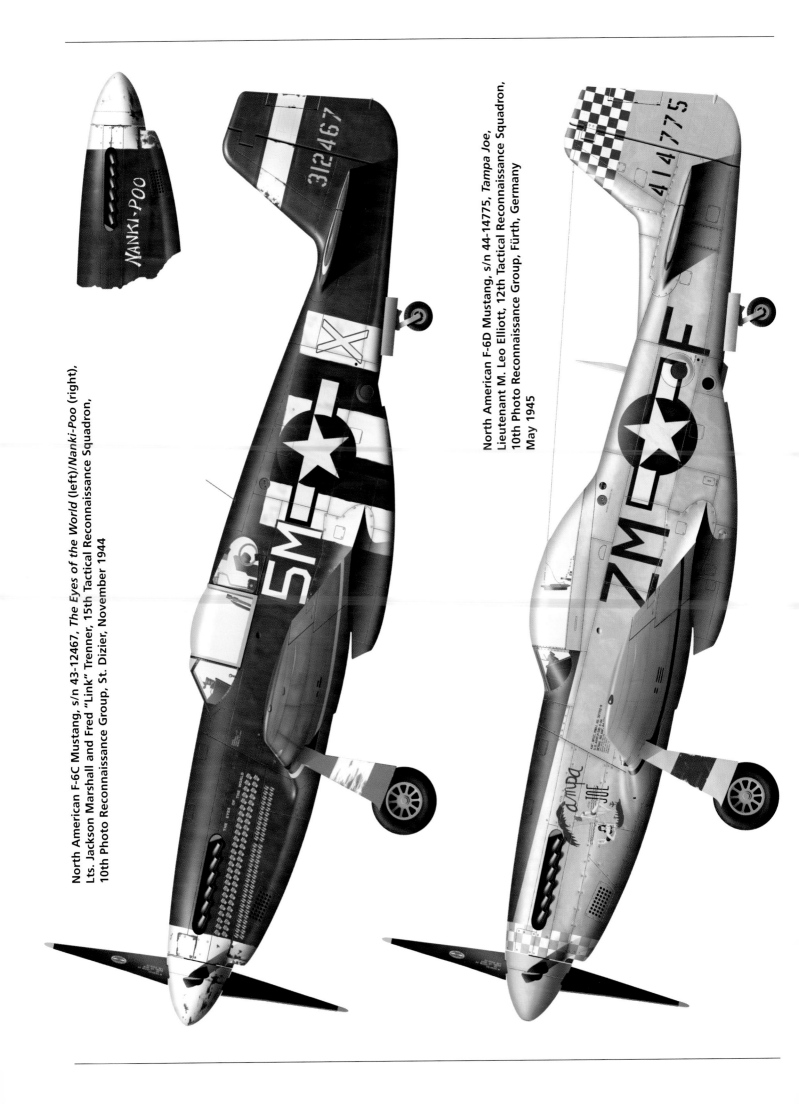

North American F-6C Mustang, s/n 43-12467, *The Eyes of the World* (left)/*Nanki-Poo* (right),
Lts. Jackson Marshall and Fred "Link" Trenner, 15th Tactical Reconnaissance Squadron,
10th Photo Reconnaissance Group, St. Dizier, November 1944

North American F-6D Mustang, s/n 44-14775, *Tampa Joe*,
Lieutenant M. Leo Elliott, 12th Tactical Reconnaissance Squadron,
10th Photo Reconnaissance Group, Fürth, Germany
May 1945

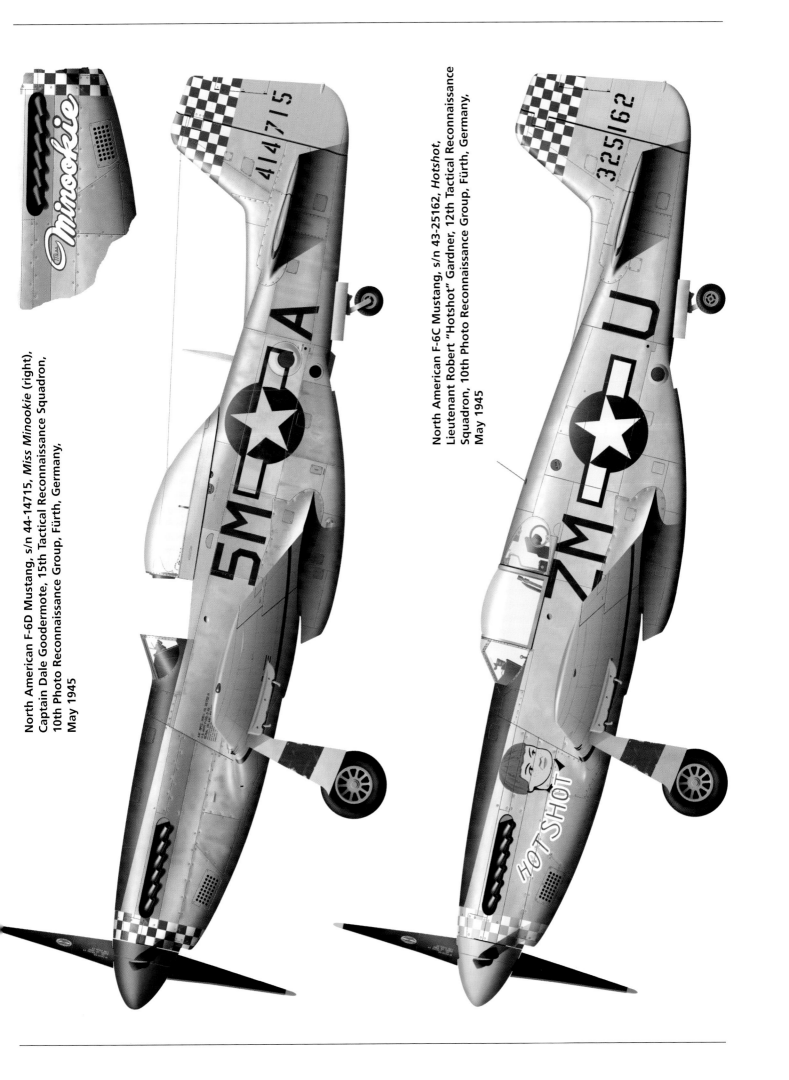

North American F-6D Mustang, s/n 44-14715, *Miss Minookie* (right),
Captain Dale Goodermote, 15th Tactical Reconnaissance Squadron,
10th Photo Reconnaissance Group, Fürth, Germany,
May 1945

North American F-6C Mustang, s/n 43-25162, *Hotshot*,
Lieutenant Robert "Hotshot" Gardner, 12th Tactical Reconnaissance
Squadron, 10th Photo Reconnaissance Group, Fürth, Germany,
May 1945

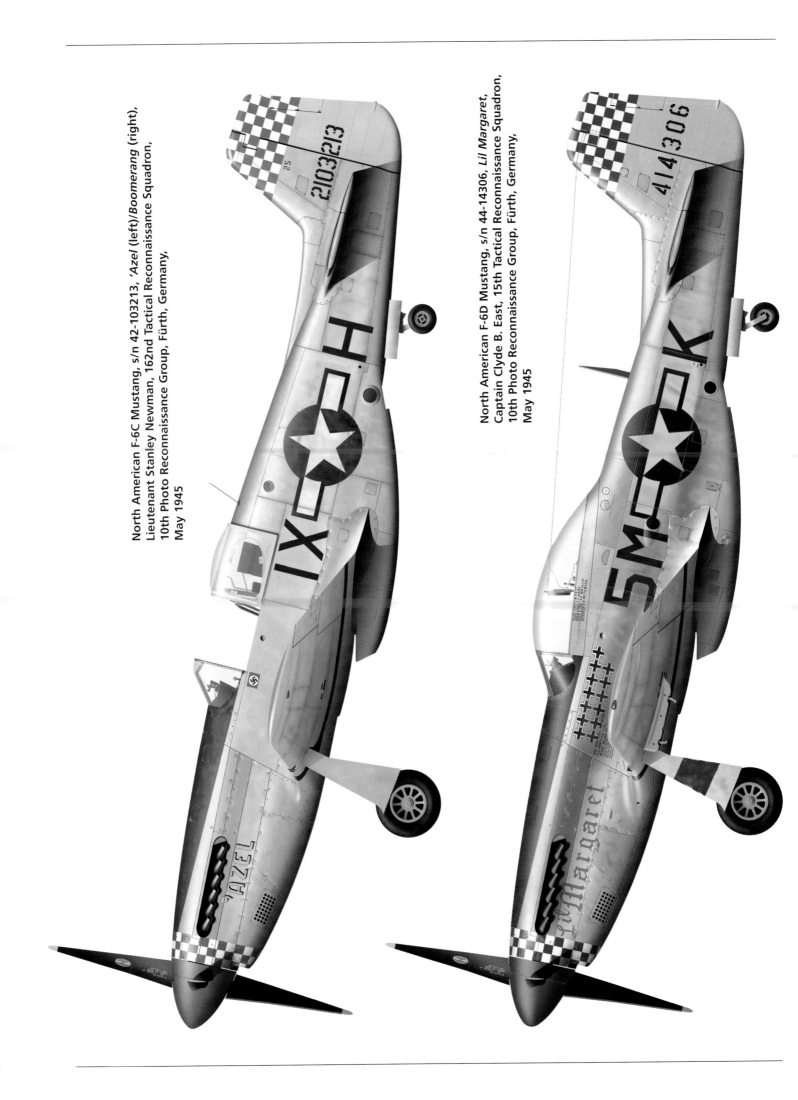

North American F-6C Mustang, s/n 42-103213, 'Azel (left)/Boomerang (right).
Lieutenant Stanley Newman, 162nd Tactical Reconnaissance Squadron,
10th Photo Reconnaissance Group, Fürth, Germany,
May 1945

North American F-6D Mustang, s/n 44-14306, Lil Margaret,
Captain Clyde B. East, 15th Tactical Reconnaissance Squadron,
10th Photo Reconnaissance Group, Fürth, Germany,
May 1945

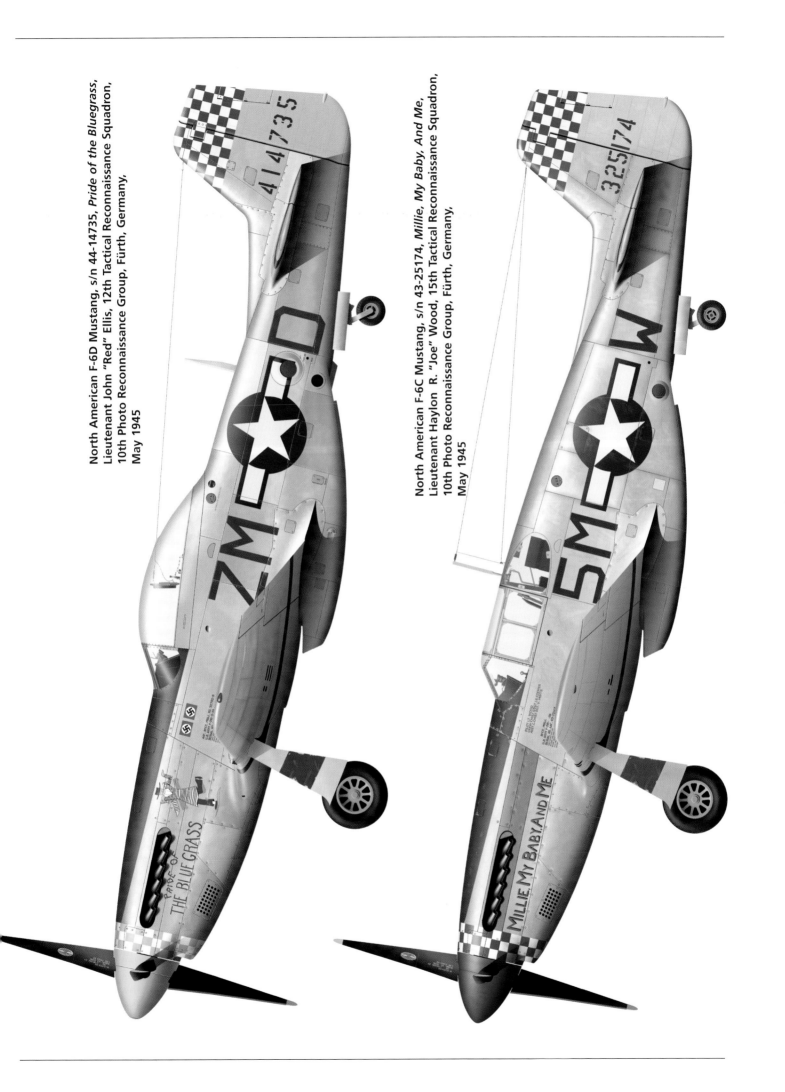

North American F-6D Mustang, s/n 44-14735, *Pride of the Bluegrass*, Lieutenant John "Red" Ellis, 12th Tactical Reconnaissance Squadron, 10th Photo Reconnaissance Group, Fürth, Germany, May 1945

North American F-6C Mustang, s/n 43-25174, *Millie, My Baby, And Me*, Lieutenant Haylon R. "Joe" Wood, 15th Tactical Reconnaissance Squadron, 10th Photo Reconnaissance Group, Fürth, Germany, May 1945

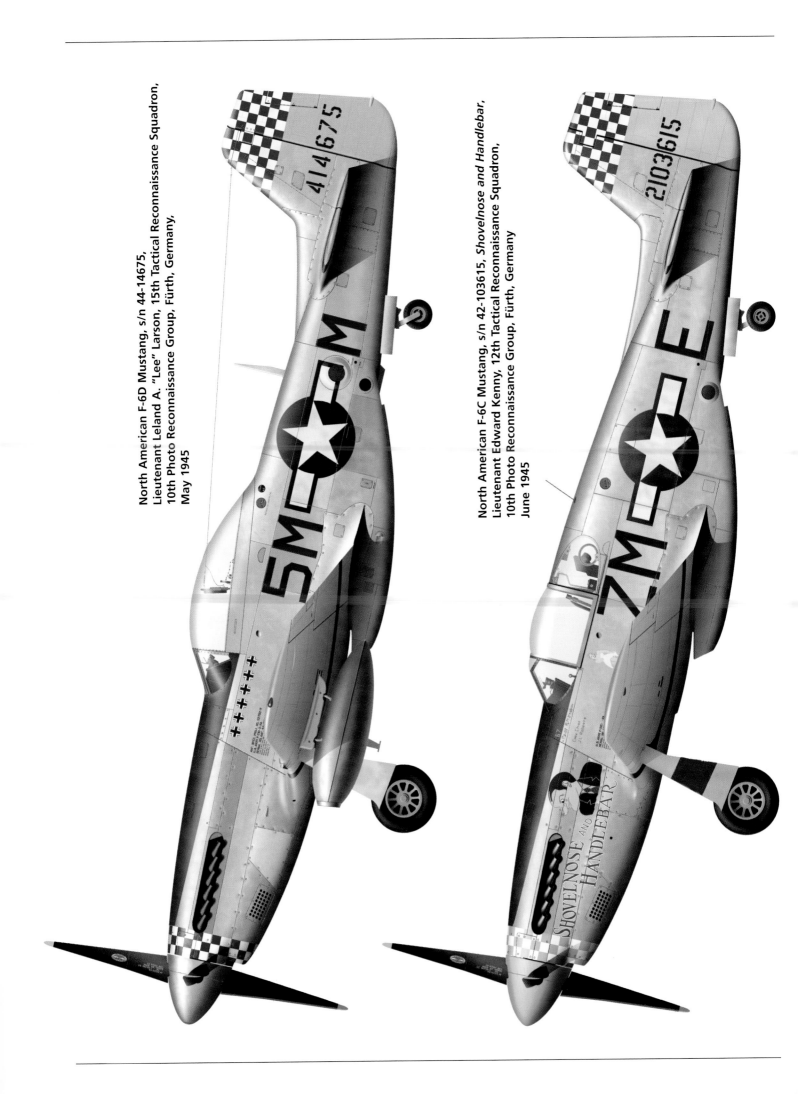

North American F-6D Mustang, s/n 44-14675,
Lieutenant Leland A. "Lee" Larson, 15th Tactical Reconnaissance Squadron,
10th Photo Reconnaissance Group, Fürth, Germany.
May 1945

North American F-6C Mustang, s/n 42-103615, *Shovelnose and Handlebar*,
Lieutenant Edward Kenny, 12th Tactical Reconnaissance Squadron,
10th Photo Reconnaissance Group, Fürth, Germany
June 1945

"I was plenty frightened, but it soon changed to anger. As my speed dropped off from 330 to 250, I saw several Jerries shooting at me and I would have given anything to have had guns to dish out some lead myself. I received fire in several places, but as they didn't hit me I didn't consider it necessary to break away from my camera run.

"After I rounded a sharp bend intense *flak* again arched up. I felt my rudders jar and I knew I had been hit again. The right engine was hot; the coolant radiator on it had been hit three times. I stayed on the deck to the last minute and pulled up over the hills with plenty of speed to spare. I got a vector to base and was soon circling the field at 300 feet with visibility about one mile. I landed OK – climbed out and patted the good right engine."

Upon landing, Captain Holbury's F-5 was a virtual wreck. Its left vertical stabilizer was shot off, large holes were in the horizontal stabilizer, and the left rudder was just hanging on. There were numerous other hits all over the aircraft, but the Lightning still managed to return Holbury to base with 212 very revealing photographs.

The photographs indicated that there was no imminent threat from the Panzer units across the Saar and that redeployment of US forces to the area was not required. For his outstanding mission Captain Holbury was awarded the Distinguished Service Cross.

The weather continued to deteriorate during the next few days and aerial operations, for all practical purposes, stopped until 10 January 1945. A slight improvement in the weather on that date allowed the 15th TRS to dispatch nine missions and its pilots reported a general lack of activity in their respective areas. During a special mission to check the road network in the Saarbrücken, Trier, and Koblenz areas Lieutenant Clyde East found only a few scattered vehicles,

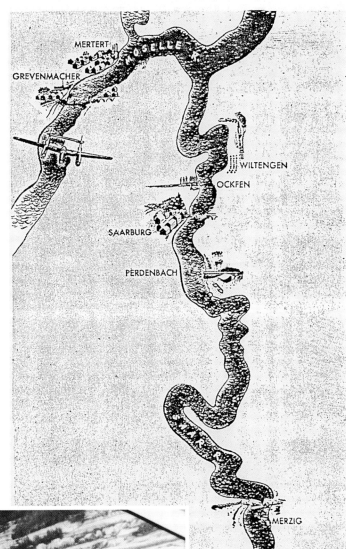

MAP OF CAPTAIN ROBERT HOLBURY'S DICING MISSION

JANUARY 5, 1945

A map taken from a Ninth Air Force intelligence report showing the route flown by Captain Robert Holbury on 5 January 1945 – from south of Merzig to the Saar-Moselle junction, westward along the Moselle.

This shot of the knocked-out bridge over the Saar River at Merzig was one of the photographs taken by Captain Holbury during his 5 January 1945 mission.
(*credit: Newton Jarrard*)

ABOVE: Sherry Ann was assigned to Lt. Claude Franklin of the 12th TRS. It was coded ZM✪Bl (bar), s/n 42-103371. (*credit: 12th TRS Assn*)

ABOVE: Lieutenant Claude Franklin and F-6C *Sherry Ann.* On its right side, the aircraft carried the name *Th-Californian* which more than likely came from Franklin's crew chief since Franklin was a native of Cincinnati, Ohio. (*credit: 12th TRS Assn*)

but did not leave the area without calling on them. In an instant Lieutenant East had his Mustang in a dive and began strafing the Germans before they could react, leaving one heavy truck burning and a wrecked motorcycle alongside the road. With continued reports coming in about a German build-up in the Saarbrücken-Neunkirchen area, Lieutenant East returned to the area on 12 and 13 January. On the second of these missions he observed several hundred troops, scattered trucks and vehicles. The sight was too much of a temptation for him to let pass. East headed to the deck and worked over the area, later recording in his logbook: "*Pranged four trucks and lots of Krauts.*"

The squadrons of the 10th PRG were kept relatively busy on 14 January, and for the 12th TRS it was a very successful day. Captain Edward L. Bishop set the stage by directing one of the most outstanding artillery adjustment missions flown by the Group. He was over a small town in Belgium directing artillery fire when he observed a long column of German armor moving into Houffalize, and immediately contacted the fighter-bombers. When the Thunderbolts arrived Captain Bishop led them to the target, but the *flak* was so intense they could not attack the column. Bishop then contacted the artillery and had them fire into the German *flak* positions. While the artillery fire kept the German *flak* gunners in their shelters, the fighter-bombers attacked and destroyed the entire column. By the time the

ABOVE: Lieutenant Mingo V. Logothetis of the 12th TRS. (*credit: Donald Lynch*)

RIGHT: This 155th NPS crew brought back the dramatic views of the marshaling yard at Stuttgart on 14 January 1945. From left to right: Lt. W. A. Wolfe (pilot) and Lt. J.G. Musal (navigator). (*credit: James Williams*)

attack was completed Bishop located some gun positions and had the artillery lay smoke markers on them. With the new targets pinpointed, the P-47s again headed toward the deck and destroyed the guns with a combination of bombs and machine gun fire.

Shortly after Captain Bishop performed his exemplary mission, Lts Mingo Logothetis and Claude Franklin of the 12th TRS were attacked by a German jet near Diekirch. The jet made a firing pass at the section from six o'clock and missed. As it pulled up into a wing-over, Lieutenant Franklin fired a burst at it. Logothetis then followed the jet into a series of diving turns and blasted pieces from its wings, canopy and left engine. As Lieutenant Logothetis broke off his firing pass he saw pieces fall away from the jet's tail section, and reported it as destroyed. (Lieutenant Logothetis reported the jet as an He 280, but since that aircraft was never used operationally, it was most probably an Me 262.)

Aerial encounters were also experienced by a section of the 15th TRS during the day but without the same success. Lts. Leland Larson and Ed Goval encountered some Fw 190s and both pilots had damaged their respective target when the guns of both Mustangs jammed just as they were closing in for the kill. Lieutenant Clyde East, however, found his targets on the ground in the form of two truck convoys, and destroyed six trucks and killed or wounded numerous German soldiers.

Lady Luck continued to smile on the Group that evening when F-3As of the 155th NPS took to the air. A mission of particular note was that flown by Lieutenant W. A. Wolfe and his crew. When they arrived over their assigned target at Kaiserslautern, it was undergoing a heavy bombing raid by the RAF and the sky was filled with *flak* and searchlight beams, so Wolfe elected to head north and look for a more promising target. After flying for a short while lights were observed on the ground, and Wolfe dropped his flash bombs and began filming the area. When his films were developed and plotted on the map it turned out that they had taken a dramatic photo of marshaling yards just north of Stuttgart. The photos revealed 1,800 goods wagons, 15 locomotives with steam up, and several trains in motion. North of the yards they had photographed 15 twin-engine and single-engine aircraft dispersed on a field thought to be vacant. The next night, 500 RAF bombers paid a visit to the scene and obliterated the marshaling yards and aircraft that Lieutenant Wolfe had found.

The 12th TRS went back into the convoy destruction business on 16 January when Lieutenant John Tillett found a convoy of 40 vehicles and called in Thunderbolts. After watching the fighter-bombers destroy this convoy, Tillett continued on and soon found a group of trucks parked in some woods and again led the Thunderbolts to the spot.

Pilots of the 15th TRS also returned with reports of German movement. Lieutenant Howard Nichols brought in a long and valuable report on 17 bridges across the

Moselle River and evidence of heavy German traffic between Trier and Bitburg. Lieutenant Clyde East of the 15th TRS along with Major John Florence, checked out the Saarbrücken, Forbach, and Neunkirchen area. They reported the marshaling yard at Neunkirchen as quite active and pinpointed a number of small convoys.

It was becoming obvious from the many reports of German road traffic that the enemy retreat was accelerating and that Patton's Third Army was maintaining pressure, especially in the St-Vith area. A second factor that was aiding the Allied push in this area was the Russian winter offensive, which was making steady gains toward Berlin. The Russian offensive made it imperative for the Germans to shift many of their Panzer units to the ever-shrinking Eastern Front in order to defend Berlin. The German retreat was favored by the return of miserable weather during the period of 19-21 January but when the weather cleared on 22 January, it spelled catastrophe for the retreating *Wehrmacht*. Hundreds of XIX TAC fighter-bombers were in the air and these aircraft, guided by the sharp-eyed pilots of the 12th and 15th Tactical Reconnaissance Squadrons, began a wholesale slaughter of German motorized units that were jamming roads.

The massacre began when Lieutenant Howard Nichols of the 15th TRS sighted a concentration of over 400 vehicles lining the roads near Dasburg. Nichols quickly notified the controller and soon afterward flight after flight of the deadly Thunderbolts bombed and strafed the column. When the attack had ended, over 300 of the vehicles in the column were burning wreckage. The devastation continued when Lieutenant Bill Brackett of the 15th TRS found another concentration of vehicles and directed artillery fire into them. Then as he approached Dasburg, he found another convoy of about 150 vehicles and directed the fighter-bombers to it.

In order to get an idea of how much damage was being done, the 31st PS was requested to fly a "dicing" mission over the area that was protected by at least ninety 88 mm

P-47s of the 354th Fighter Group, each laden with bombs and eight .50 caliber machine guns, taxi out for a mission to the "Bulge," January 1945. (*credit: Air Force Museum*)

flak guns. Lieutenant Thair W. Best volunteered for the mission and took off at 15.28 hrs to obtain the photographs. Upon arrival in the area Best circled and then began his photo run. His Lightning was less than half way through its run when it was hit repeatedly by flak, burst into flames and crashed. Somehow Lieutenant Best survived the shootdown and finished out the war as a POW. Later in the day the ceiling lifted enough to permit Lieutenant Ray Krone to photograph the area from 16,000 ft and his photos confirmed the reported slaughter.

The aerial assault on the retreating Germans continued the next day. Lieutenant Clyde East of the 15th TRS reported several concentrations of vehicles north-east of Vianden, including one consisting of over 2,000 vehicles. East contacted two flights of P-47s and led them to the target. In the attack Lieutenant East personally destroyed four trucks and then watched as the Thunderbolts clobbered another 50 before he left the scene. His logbook entry for the day read, "Best mission yet!"

Before the day ended the Thunderbolt pilots from the 362nd, 368th, 354th, and 365th Fighter Groups claimed 317 motor transports destroyed and 168 damaged; 20 tanks and other armored vehicles destroyed; and 11 horse-drawn vehicles destroyed. In addition to the destruction of the convoy the Thunderbolt pilots also laid waste to 12 gun positions and other miscellaneous targets around Vianden.

To assist in the convoy attacks Ninth Bomber Command dispatched some of its new Douglas A-26 Invaders against these targets. For the 416th Bomb Group it was a disaster. Just before noon on 23 January Lieutenant Howard Nichols of the 15th TRS made rendezvous with five A-26s of the 670th Bomb Squadron over Luxembourg and led them to the targets. After Nichols pointed out the target the Invaders began their attack on the convoy and were quickly repulsed by extremely heavy and accurate flak. Two of the A-26s were crippled by the flak and made it back to Allied held territory before crash-landing.

Lieutenant Nichols then returned to Luxembourg and met six Invaders of the 671st BS and led them back to Dasburg for another try at the convoy. While en route to the target, Nichols guided the bombers around flak positions and then personally damaged six trucks as he led them in an attack against a convoy of 75 trucks. The A-26s followed and the lead ship was sent down in flames by flak. Seconds later another A-26 was shot out of the sky. The third Invader received serious damage to its left

One of the 15th TRS's most outstanding pilots and leaders was Captain Howard Nichols. Nichols flew many successful missions before his death on 18 March 1945 when his Mustang collided with high tension cables near Merl, Germany. (credit: Robert Dawson)

wing and Lieutenant Nichols escorted it back to Luxembourg. The other three A-26s escaped the flak barrage undamaged.

The results of the A-26 attacks had been a disaster, but Ninth Air Force operations as a whole were extremely successful. Its aircraft had reaped a harvest of German equipment that exceeded the destruction at the Falaise Gap.

On the ground, American troops had recaptured St-Vith on 23 January and within the next few days the Third Army had cleared the "Skyline Drive" which overlooked the Prüm valley from St. Vith to Diekirch. By 28 January American forces had regained the original positions held by the First Army at the time of the German breakthrough.

After a very productive month in the air all the officers and enlisted men of the 10th Photo Reconnaissance Group were assembled on its airstrip during the early hours of 29 January to take on another enemy. A deep snow had covered the area and from Colonel Russ Berg on down, the men struggled in sub-zero weather to clear the runway in preparation for upcoming operations.

While the 10th PRG was clearing snow, the Third Army was beginning its assault in the Eifel to destroy German Army Group G. From positions in the St-Vith area three of George Patton's divisions crossed the flooding Our River and headed toward Prüm, a communications center which was the key to the German northern Eifel defenses. By the end of the day his infantrymen had cleared five fortified villages and pushed two miles into Germany.

Lieutenant Arnold Meyer was flying this aircraft (5M✪N) when he was shot down by Fw 190s on 13 February 1945. (*credit: Robert Dawson*)

On 15 February both tactical reconnaissance squadrons were up in force and flew a mixture of front line coverage, route reconnaissance, and artillery adjustment missions. Their reports indicated that the Germans were trying desperately to defend their positions along the Third Army front. Captain Edward Bishop and Lieutenant Henry Ermatinger, of the 12th TRS, for example, encountered *flak* at several points during their visual reconnaissance of the Trier-Prüm-Walsfeld area. Captain John Hoefker and Lieutenant Clyde East flew deeper into Germany and noted heavy rail traffic in and around the towns of Ludwigshafen, Mannheim, Heidelberg and Würzburg. Another mission of note was flown by Captain Bob Dawson of the 15th TRS. With his wingman, Lieutenant Stewart Wilson, covering his tail, Captain Dawson brought down artillery fire on a serviceable bridge over the Saar River and left it in ruins.

The 15th TRS flew 17 missions during the day, most of which were long route reconnaissance missions covering roads and rail lines, and all of the pilots brought back detailed reports of German traffic and troop positions. There was one tragic exception to an otherwise successful day. Near Kaiserslautern a gaggle of 15 Fw 190s swooped down out of the sun and attacked Captain Bob Dawson and Lieutenant Arnold Meyer. The bounce was so successful that Lieutenant Meyer was shot out of the sky before he could even react to the attack. By some skillful maneuvering Captain Dawson was able to evade the German fighters but was unable to get a fix on the spot where Lieutenant Meyer went down.

The 31st PS also had an extremely busy day, flying 36 bomb damage assessment missions to a number of points deep into Germany. Their missions covered both Eighth and Ninth Air Force bombing raids. Lieutenant Russell Mykyten accompanied a group of B-26s to the Ruhr Valley and observed the attack and photographed the results, while Lieutenant Ray Krone was doing the same for medium bombers striking targets at Euskirchen, Trier, Frankfurt, and Koblenz. Lieutenant Dan Davis on the other hand, accompanied Eighth AF B-17s to Bonn and observed the attack before heading over the city for BDA photographs. This target was heavily defended by *flak* and enemy aircraft, but Davis completed his run and returned to base with excellent photographs.

On the ground, Patton's Third Army continued its "probe" of the German defenses and was making headway in its "creeping defensive" into the Eifel. Attacking from the east and south of Prüm, VIII Corps pushed nine miles into the German lines and XXII Corps struck northward and advanced halfway to Bitburg. With

Captain Bob Dawson of the 15th TRS. (*credit: Robert Dawson*)

At some point in early 1945, 5M◉Y, s/n 44-14101, was converted into a two-seat Mustang by its crew chief, S/Sgt. Eugene Demaris. Here, its pilot, Lieutenant "Bunny" Hughes is about to take a passenger up for a flight over the lines. (*credit: Eugene Demaris*)

these advances, the Third Army formed a semi-circle around German troops between Prüm and Echternach. During the next four days it squeezed this pocket of resistance even tighter and by 24 February, the Third Army was beginning to close in on Bitburg.

During this period the 12th and 15th Tactical Reconnaissance Squadrons flew numerous artillery adjustment missions in support of Patton's march into the Eifel. The missions of 21 February saw some excellent artillery adjustment work and Lieutenant Henry Lacey of the 15th TRS led P-47s in a successful attack on a small convoy.

Both tactical reconnaissance squadrons were up in force on 23 February and it was a day mixed with success and frustration. The day began on a positive note with Lts. Gilbert Nicklas and Wallace Mitchell of the 12th TRS noting the presence of a number of trains in the Trier marshaling yards and pinpointing a prisoner-of-war camp on the outskirts of town. Acting on this report and other data, pilots of the 15th TRS then directed a number of devastating artillery barrages into German positions. Lts. Eugene Balachowski and Richard McFadden targeted a concentration of tanks and troops

while Lieutenant Clyde East directed fire for an hour and a half into the Trier marshaling yards. Another 15th TRS pilot, Lieutenant Norbert Kirkpatrick, located an excellent target for the fighter-bombers, but when he made contact with a flight of 20 P-47s, they refused to follow him to the target and one of them tried to shoot him down!

The worst error in recognition of the day occurred while Lts. Donald Dowell and Floyd Lofland of the 15th TRS were flying a route reconnaissance in the vicinity of

ZM◉F seen following a rough mission during which its right wing tip was shot off. Its pilot, Major John Florence was able, after some frightening moments, to nurse his damaged aircraft back to base and make a safe landing. (*credit: John Florence*)

Major John Florence, CO of the 12th TRS, poses with the 15th TRS's F-6C, 5M✪X, *The Eyes of the World/Nanki-Poo* at St. Dizier. (*credit: Ralph Woolner*)

The new day brought no relief for the battered Germans as the Third and Seventh Armies continued to pressure them on the ground and XIX TAC struck them from above. On this date, 17 March 1945, the fighter-bombers of XIX TAC scored a record kill by destroying or damaging 1,033 motor vehicles, 416 horse-drawn vehicles, 176 tanks and armored vehicles, 69 locomotives, and 588 railcars. Tactical reconnaissance pilots were also kept quite busy locating and directing the fighter-bombers throughout this aerial siege. Captain John Hoefker joined Lieutenant Bill Davenport of the 12th TRS on a long visual reconnaissance mission that took them to the Worms, Bad Kreuznach and Bingen areas. During the mission they spotted a convoy of 40 vehicles and directed P-47s to the site. At about the same time two other sections of the 12th TRS were checking out the countryside in and around the cities of Frankfurt, Koblenz, and St. Wendel. Lieutenant Leon Canady noted German roadblocks on the road to Kirchberg and numerous barges on the river. Major John Florence, who assumed command of the 12th TRS in February, and Captain Ed Bishop reported that American troops were entering Bad Kreuznach, and observed a three mile-long zigzag trench at Worms. Lts. Don Lynch and Melvin Strange played a major role in the events of the day. After completing their artillery adjustment

mission, the section was starting home when they noticed the beginnings of a German retreat from the town of Immeldorf. Lynch called in the co-ordinates to the artillery and his fire direction was deadly accurate. The first round landed at the head of the German column and caused numerous casualties and panic among the survivors.

The 15th TRS also enjoyed a very successful day but lost two aircraft and an outstanding pilot. The first loss occurred when Lieutenant Norbert Kirkpatrick was forced to crash-land his Mustang about 20 miles south of Luxembourg when his engine failed. The second and most serious loss of the day happened near Merl, Germany when Captain Howard Nichols collided with high-tension wires and was killed.

On the plus side of the ledger the 15th TRS added two more confirmed kills and two probables to its scoreboard. Lts. Norborne Thomas and Guy Cary were in the process of checking for activity at an airfield near Hanau when the section was bounced by eight Bf 109s and two Fw 190s. Thomas turned into the Bf 109s, fired a long burst, and observed strikes all over the first Bf 109. The stricken enemy aircraft first went into a snap roll and then dove straight into the ground and exploded. Lieutenant Thomas then turned his attention to another Bf 109 and scored hits all over its fuselage and tail section. He last observed this aircraft as it was heading earthward trailing a plume of heavy black smoke. Cary then took over and attacked another of the Bf 109s. His first burst scored numerous hits on the enemy aircraft's engine and fuselage and the Bf 109 went into a dive. Lieutenant Cary followed it down and observed it crash into a grove of trees and explode. As he began to climb for altitude, Cary opened fire on a passing Fw 190 and his well-placed burst hit its engine and it began to trail white smoke. Cary did not see this Fw 190 crash and was forced to claim it as a probable.

The 31st PS flew 16 missions on 18 March and covered the Frankfurt, Darmstadt, Koblenz, and Bingen areas. The photos produced by these pilots provided

The end of 5M✪X, s/n 43-12467. The former *The Eyes of the World/Nanki-Poo* is stripped of usable parts after she was crash-landed on 17 March 1945 by Lt. Norbert Kirkpatrick. (*credit: 15th TRS Assn*)

5M⊙V, s/n 42-103311, *The Insect* seen at Trier, Germany in March 1945. (*credit: Hal Edwards*)

photographs of every mile of its planned advance were needed and the 31st PS was called upon to produce low-level photographs of the roads. These photo runs would not be on-the-deck "dicing" runs as undertaken in Normandy; instead, the pilots would fly at the more vulnerable altitude of 5,000 ft and photograph every foot of road with their nose cameras. The one safety factor in the Normandy "dicing" missions was that they were flown at such low altitudes that it was difficult for gunners to bring their guns to bear, but at 5,000 ft the aircraft would face danger from *flak* and enemy fighters alike.

excellent images of the German defenses in the region. The photos also revealed that the airfields in the area had been heavily damaged by Allied bombing raids.

The Third Army battering ram broke through the German defenses and demonstrated its mobility by overrunning 950 square miles on 19 March 1945, virtually eliminating organized German resistance in the Palatinate area. With so much territory changing hands so quickly, Patton's "aerial eyes" remained over the area continuously to keep commanders up to date on the highly fluid situation, and to locate targets for the fighter-bombers. During his mission, Major John Florence of the 12th TRS noted eight bridges that were still intact along the Nahe River and some contrasting actions of German troops in the area. As he flew over Bad Kreuznach, he observed US troops taking the surrender of hundreds of white flag-waving Germans; a few moments later he saw other Germans building roadblocks outside of Alzey. While flying in the same general area Lts. Henri Lefebure and Robert Marple of the 12th TRS located two separate convoys, one containing about 50 vehicles and the second containing over 500, and directed fighter-bombers to both targets. Before leaving the area, the section observed 28 Thunderbolts attacking the large convoy and turning it into a blazing inferno. Next to arrive on the scene were Lts. Ron Ricci and Bill Davenport of the 12th TRS and this duo located four more convoys for the deadly P-47s.

With speed and surprise playing a major role in Patton's success during the breakout, he intended to use Germany's famed *autobahn* system to accelerate his advance. However, in order for the Third Army to make proper use of the *autobahn*, detailed

The first "dicing" mission down the *autobahn* was flown on 19 March by Lieutenant Russell Mykyten, who volunteered for the assignment, which covered the stretch between Kaiserslautern and the River Rhine. Mykyten solved the problem of defense by diving from 12,000 ft to 5,000 ft and then streaking down the *autobahn* at more than 400 mph. The remarkable photos he brought back enabled the 10th Armored Division to complete its push to the Rhine in record time and earned Lieutenant Mykyten the Distinguished Flying Cross. In fact, the mission was so impressive to commanders in the field that the squadron received many requests for similar photographs of almost all of the major highways in central Germany.

Four pilots of the 12th TRS. Standing, left to right: Lts. Robert Marple and Mingo Logothetis. On the wing left to right: Lts. Henri Lefebure and Bill Davenport. (*credit: William Davenport*)

9

"DUCK SOUP"

Across the Rhine to Victory: February to March 1945

The 10th PRG covered the battlefield on 20 and 21 March and assisted in the Third Army's race to cut off the German escape routes across the Rhine and to close its Rhineland campaign. Patton's forces then stormed and captured the cities of Mainz, Lugwigshafen, and Worms before barricading the Rhine between Worms and Mannheim, ending its fantastic 11 day campaign with a magnificent victory.

All three of the Group's squadrons were active on 21 March. While the 31st PS was busy photographing the territory on both sides of the Rhine for the Third Army, the tactical reconnaissance squadron covered the activities of German troops and traffic in the battle area. Lts. Claude Franklin and "Dusty" Rhodes of the 12th TRS first checked out the bridges between Ludwigshafen and Mannheim and found them to be unserviceable and then turned their attention to other targets. Upon reaching the city of Mannheim they found a marshaling yard full of railcars and directed the fighter-bombers to the target. Lts. Mingo Logothetis and Bill Davenport also found a very lucrative target and called in P-47s to hammer a huge convoy of tanks, halftracks and self–propelled artillery.

The *Luftwaffe* was up in force during the day and its fighters tried unsuccessfully to intercept several of the 31st PS's F-5 Lightnings. Other enemy aircraft tried to interfere with the tactical reconnaissance Mustangs and one of them paid for its aggressiveness when it entered the airspace occupied by Captain Clyde East and Lieutenant Leland Larson. As the section passed over a long-nosed Fw 190 D, Captain East turned and made a diving pass at the enemy aircraft but his bullets missed their target. Lieutenant Larson then jumped into a firing position and with a long burst sent the enemy aircraft to its doom. Apparently his gunfire killed the pilot because as soon as it was hit the Focke-Wulf went over into a slow roll and dived straight into the ground. As the future Ace began to climb for altitude after scoring his first victory, East spotted ten more Fw 190s coming in and radioed a warning for Larson to head for the deck and escape. The two Mustangs skimmed along the deck and easily outran the pursuing Fw 190s, then pulled up and continued their mission.

While these aerial activities were taking place, Generals Omar Bradley, George S. Patton, and Courtney Hodges were discussing plans for crossing the Rhine River and their decision was that the Third Army should cross first. Patton quickly put the plan into action and on the night of 22/23 March 1945 he sent troops of the 5th Division across at Oppenheim; a spearhead headed toward Kassel, and another for Limburg to meet up with the First Army, completely surprising the German defenders. By nightfall of 24 March, the Third Army had crossed the Rhine at four points, and by the end of the day on 26 March, it had captured Darmstadt and Aschaffenburg and had encircled Frankfurt.

With the Third Army waging war in three directions; – mopping up in the Palatinate, a spearhead making toward Kassel, and another for Limburg to meet up with the First Army – the 10th PRG was kept well-occupied.

On 24 March the Group's tactical reconnaissance squadrons had a busy day, engaging enemy aircraft in aerial dogfights and directing the fighter-bombers to fat

BELOW: The 10th PRG's "Ace of Aces", Captain Clyde B. East of the 15th TRS. East had achieved 13 victories by the end of the war. (credit: Robert Dawson)

BELOW RIGHT: Lt. Leland A. "Lee" Larson of the 15th TRS became the 10th PRG's third-ranking Ace with six victories. (credit: William N. Hess)

targets on the ground. Early that morning six Bf 109s bounced Captain Clyde East and Lieutenant Lee Larson of the 15th TRS near Eisenach. The Bf 109s attacked from out of the sun, but the section made a 180 degree turn to the left and caught two of the German fighters as they tried to follow them into the turn. East and Larson chose their respective targets and opened fire almost simultaneously, with devastating results. East's Bf 109 exploded in mid-air and pieces from it slightly damaged his Mustang, while Larson's victim spun downward and exploded upon impact with the earth. After they climbed back to 7,000 ft Captain East observed another Bf 109 as it was slipping into firing position on Larson's tail. East quickly latched onto it and blasted it out of the sky. This victory was Captain East's fifth kill and he became the Squadron's second Ace.

Lieutenant Haylon R. Wood found a train near Neustadt pulling 15 flatcars loaded with tanks and led a squadron of Thunderbolts to the attack. As Wood made the first pass he received *flak* that was so intense that the

General George S. Patton. during the crossing of the Rhine River in March 1945. (*credit: 15th TRS Assn*)

P-47s refused to follow him and flew off in search of less hostile targets. Lieutenant Chuck Rowland was a little more fortunate. He led another squadron of P-47s against a convoy of 300 vehicles and watched as the Thunderbolts ripped it apart. On his second mission of the day, Wood provided more targets for the Thunderbolts and led them on two separate attacks. The first target was a concentration of 75 vehicles near Wiesbaden and the second was an airfield near Limburg. In the latter attack Lieutenant Wood destroyed an Fw 190 on the ground.

These unrelenting aerial assaults led by tactical reconnaissance pilots continued throughout the remainder of March and resulted in tremendous damage to the crumbling German war machine. On 26 March the 15th TRS flew 16 more of these successful missions. Captain Al Frick and Lts. Lee Larson and Henry Lacey each led attacks against large convoys and witnessed their destruction, but the greatest target of the day was found by Lieutenant Wood. Wood related his mission: "My

BELOW: Lt. Larson chats with his crew chief just before starting his engine and heading out for a mission from Trier, March 1945. (*credit: Amos Christianson*)

HEADQUARTERS
THIRD UNITED STATES ARMY
APO 403

GENERAL ORDERS   23 March 1945

NUMBER   70

TO THE OFFICERS AND MEN OF THE THIRD ARMY

AND

TO OUR COMRADES OF THE XIX TACTICAL AIR COMMAND

In the period from January 29 to March 22, 1945, you have wrested 6,484 square miles of territory from the enemy. You have taken 3,072 cities, towns, and villages, including among the former: TRIER, KOBLENZ, BINGEN, WORMS, MAINZ, KAISERSLAUTERN, and LUDWIGSHAFEN.

You have captured 140,112 enemy soldiers, and have killed or wounded an additional 99,000, thereby eliminating practically all of the German 7th and 1st Armies. History records no greater achievement in so limited a time.

This great campaign was only made possible by your disciplined valor, unswerving devotion to duty, coupled with the unparalleled audacity and speed of your advance on the ground; while from the air, the peerless fighter-bombers kept up a relentless round-the-clock attack upon the disorganized enemy.

The world rings with your praises: better still, General Marshall, General Eisenhower, and General Bradley have all personally commended you. The highest honor I have ever attained is that of having my name coupled with yours in these great events.

Please accept my heartfelt admiration and thanks for what you have done, and remember that your assault crossing over the Rhine at 2200 hours last night assures you of even greater glory to come.

G. S. PATTON, JR.
Lieut. General, U. S. Army,
Commanding.

DISTRIBUTION:
"A" & "C"
Twelfth Army Group
XIX TAC

wingman was Lieutenant William Webb and our mission was to recce the Remagen bridgehead and the areas around and beyond it. Visibility was unlimited on this beautiful day and as we approached the area I immediately realized things were happening. That our forces had broken out was apparent; that the breakout had only occurred a short time before our arrival was apparent; that this was a field day for our forces was quite soon to be a fact, a reality. A relatively small town (Limburg) – but a key communications center – was located only a few miles east of the bridgehead. From this point some half dozen roads radiated generally eastward. Our troops and armor were fanning out along each road, preceded by bedraggled groups composed of German troops and civilians. I was amazed that such an enormous operation was taking place in

Major Lyon L. Davis' *The Sandspur* photographed by Lieutenant Stewart Wilson over Germany, Spring 1945. (*credit: Stewart Wilson*)

the absence of massive air assistance, no US or Allied aircraft were in the area. My amazement was confirmed when I contacted Central Control, for neither was that center aware of such an undertaking. With overcharged elation I apparently convinced Central Control that "the war can be ended here today." Please send every squadron of P-47s that you have available.

"Within moments my conversation with Central Control made it apparent that word was spreading, an onslaught was in progress. Central assured that P-47s were on their way from virtually every point of the compass, and nine squadrons were to arrive before my departure. As they began to come in I informed them, incorrectly, that

there was no *flak*. I had strafed an enemy column prior to the arrival of the first P-47 squadron and had led that squadron on its first pass and no *flak* was encountered. That my first assessment of "no *flak*" was in error was soon to become evident. Upon the arrival of the third or fourth squadron I led the strafing run and as I pulled up and banked sharply to the left, the sky was suddenly filled with 20 mm and 40 mm "golf balls." Scared and angered by the *flak* that had passed dangerously close, I turned and dived into the line of fire and began a strafing pass which I have regretted ever since. I rolled out at 50 feet and pressed the trigger, sending streams of .50 caliber fire into the mass of people in the road before I realized a white banner was being waved by civilians mixed in with the German soldiers. I quickly released the trigger, but it was too late to undo the damage."

As Lieutenant Wood pulled up and over this column, the fighter-bombers continued to strike the numerous retreating columns and when the attack was completed over 200 German vehicles had been put out of action.

The destruction of German convoys continued on 25 March. Captain Clyde East led Thunderbolts to a column of 45 trucks at Idstein and saw 15 of them engulfed in flames before he departed the scene. Lts. James Webb and Haylon Wood found another large concentration of approximately 400 vehicles parked bumper to bumper near Wetzlar and led fighter-bombers in an attack that destroyed approximately 200 of them

Lieutenant Alfred O. Frick's F-6K *Kitten*, 5M✪X, s/n 44-12812. This photograph was taken in April 1945 after the 10th PRG moved to Fürth, Germany. (*credit: Fred Remian*)

and set nearby woods alight. Lieutenant Richard McFadden, also of the 15th TRS, found another 1,100 vehicles in his area and observed the destruction of 100 before he headed back to base.

The *Luftwaffe* did not escape the wrath of the 15th TRS either. Lts. Wayne Patrick and Lee Larson chased a Bf 109 back toward its own lines and saw it shot down by German *flak* gunners, and Captain Clyde East and Lieutenant Henry Lacey turned an abortive reconnaissance mission into a very successful fighter attack. Captain East reported: "We ran into bad weather and were returning from our route when seven Ju 87 Stukas were observed dive bombing (our troops) in the town of Hammelburg. We were at 2,000 feet when we attacked the Ju 87s which scattered as we approached. I (Captain East) got on the tail of one enemy aircraft which took violent evasive action. After several bursts I observed strikes on the left gas tank and radiator and the enemy aircraft began streaming coolant. The canopies suddenly flew open and its crew jumped and landed very near where their plane crashed. I then closed on a second Stuka and fired a three second burst and missed, and the enemy aircraft dove steeply for the deck and jettisoned its bombs. He then proceeded west on the deck and I followed, firing several deflection bursts that hit him in the landing gear and engine. Shortly afterwards the enemy aircraft started trailing smoke and coolant and its pilot took it in for a crash landing. I took photos of both aircraft after they crashed.

"Lieutenant Lacey attacked a third Ju 87 and it dove vertically, jettisoned its bombs, and pulled out on the deck. A long chase ensued with the Stuka taking violent evasive action and Lieutenant Lacey firing several short bursts from various angles and observing hits on its tail section and tail. On his next-to-last burst Lieutenant Lacey saw coolant start streaming back when his shells hit the Stuka's engine and cockpit area, and then it went into a shallow dive and crashed into some woods. The rear gunner in the Stuka continued firing all the way in."

The second of two Ju 87s shot down by Captain Clyde B. East on 27 March 1945. (credit: Clyde B. East)

Clyde East's 5M⊙K parked at Trier and displaying seven "kill" markings which reflect his victories to 27 March 1945. This photograph also reveals the second phase of the evolution of his personal markings; the name *Lil Margaret* is now displayed in small script above the exhaust pipes. (credit: Clyde B. East)

Wiesbaden was seized by the 80th Division on 28 March and the First Army's crack 9th Armored Division raced 25 miles south of Limburg where it linked up with the 80th Division, thereby cutting off a large pocket of German troops and capturing 8,000 of them in the process.

XIX Tactical Air Command also had a rewarding day as its fighter-bombers destroyed or damaged over 1,500 German vehicles. Many of these targets were found by the roving Mustangs of the 12th and 15th Tactical Reconnaissance Squadrons. The 15th flew nine missions and reported roads full of military and civilian equipment. Lieutenant Henry Lewis located 1,000 vehicles in a column and called in P-47s, but they could not bomb or strafe because of a large number of civilians within the column. Lts. Alfred Reed and Henri Lefebure of the 12th TRS, on the other hand, found a large convoy near Bad Homburg and directed an attack which virtually decimated it. Lts. Don Lynch and Elmer Olson of the 12th TRS, operating in the vicinity of Hammelburg, noted a small American convoy heading through the city toward Diekirch or the POW camp at Hammelburg. More than likely they were witnessing George Patton's attempt to liberate the camp where his son-in-law was held as a POW.

In the day's aerial action, four Bf 109s attempted to bounce Lts. "Lee" Larson and Robert Landers of the 15th TRS and paid dearly for their efforts. The section broke to the right as the Bf 109s attacked and Lieutenant Larson hit one of the enemy aircraft with a deflection shot as it passed by him. The enemy aircraft immediately began trailing a column of black smoke as it tried to escape into some clouds. Lieutenant Landers cut off the enemy aircraft's escape route and sent a fatal barrage of .50 caliber fire into the Bf 109's cockpit. With a dead man at the controls the enemy aircraft rolled over and dived straight to earth and exploded.

A second encounter took place near Maulbach, as Lts. Wayne Patrick and Henry Lacey of the 15th TRS were returning home from a very successful target-finding mission. Along the route the section encountered a lone Ju 87 Stuka and Lacey dived after it, opening fire when he

"...could see the whites of the gunner's eyes." After feeling the impact of Lacey's gunfire the Stuka's pilot bailed out at 300 ft but his parachute did not open. The rear gunner rode the stricken plane and continued firing as it plunged to earth.

The weather shut down the Group's operations for the next two days and offered the opportunity to the 12th and 31st Squadrons to move to Trier and rejoin the 15th TRS. For the 12th TRS the move was a case of history repeating itself. The Squadron had operated from this airfield during the First World War and it was only the first step in a series of moves that were nearly identical to the path it had followed in that earlier conflict.

Frankfurt fell on 29 March and the Third Army's powerful armored and infantry forces broke out in all directions. The 6th Armored Division and the 65th and 80th Infantry Divisions thrust 45 miles north-east of the city to the vicinity of Kassel. In doing so, the Third Army completed the longest and fastest of its many breakthroughs – 100 miles in less than three days. In simultaneous moves the 4th Armored and 90th Infantry Divisions pushed 25 miles to Hersfeld, and the 11th Armored and 26th Infantry Divisions advanced to Fulda.

Tactical reconnaissance closed out the month by flying more target-seeking missions and met with some success. Lts. Bob Bruce and Bob Little of the 12th TRS located numerous trains in several marshaling yards in the Hersfeld area, and watched as the Thunderbolts struck many of the railcars they had reported. Lieutenant

5M✪U *Alma* was assigned to Lieutenant Raymond Montes, Jr. of the 15th TRS. *(credit: Stewart Wilson)*

"Dusty" Rhodes had the bad luck of finding a "fat" target in the Gotha area but being unable to contact any P-47s to strike the marshaling yard that was jammed full of flatcars carrying tanks and armored vehicles. As the day continued Lieutenant "Lee" Larson found another large concentration of troops and vehicles near Wurzburg and directed an attack that laid waste to most of the 100 vehicles and killed a great number of German troops.

Perhaps the most unusual incident of the day occurred during Captain John Hoefker's mission. He and Lieutenant Charles White were flying a route

ZM✪O, s/n 44-14550, of the 12th TRS. Note the two oblique camera ports just forward of the letter O. *(credit: 12th TRS Assn)*

ABOVE: *Sugar Train*, ZMJS, s/n 44-14565, was assigned to Lieutenant Earl Miner of the 12th TRS. (credit: William Davenport)

Little was accomplished during the next two days due to deteriorating weather, so the 12th and 15th Tactical Reconnaissance Squadrons used the time to make the move to the new base at Ober-Olm, which was situated a few miles from Mainz. After the pleasant accommodation the squadrons had enjoyed at Giraumont and Trier-Evren, Ober-Olm was disappointing. There was a grass runway and no hangars or support buildings.

After establishing itself on the 50-mile north/south corridor into eastern Germany, the Third Army was ordered to limit its operations so that the First and Ninth Armies could catch up and begin a consolidated push to close the Ruhr pocket. Naturally Patton objected to the slowdown and as he predicted, German defenses stiffened and the enemy even launched limited counter-attacks. In conjunction with the stiffening German defense on the ground, the *Luftwaffe* also began to make its presence known in the area and a number of air battles ensued. The series of aerial engagements began on 4 April when pilots of the 10th PRG shot down seven enemy aircraft, and continued for several more days. The 15th TRS claimed three of the victories scored on 4 April, the first of which was scored by Captain Clyde East and

reconnaissance in the vicinity of Eisnach when he spied a German liaison aircraft in its take-off climb. Captain Hoefker whipped his Mustang around in a turn right in front of the aircraft and when he looked back the aircraft had crashed. Apparently his prop wash had flipped the light aircraft over at a low altitude and sent it into the ground. Hoefker was officially credited with the destruction of an Hs 126, but more than likely it was a Fieseler Storch. This unique kill raised Captain Hoefker's total to 8.5 victories.

April 1945 began with the Third Army engaged in hard fighting as it continued its three-pronged attack at Fulda, Hersfeld, and Kassel, but by 4 April these cities had been captured and a 50-mile corridor into eastern Germany opened. Tactical reconnaissance continued its target-finding missions in support of the Third Army and although targets were becoming fewer and smaller, they exploited every opportunity to destroy them. The 31st PS's mission continued to be photo coverage of the breakout area and usable roads and highways within the area.

The weather on 1 April was poor and observations were limited but some tactical reconnaissance sections reported movement of German armor and support vehicles, and an advance column of American armor in the vicinity of Aschaffenburg. A perfect and very timely example of air support was performed by Lieutenant Dale Goodermote of the 15th TRS when he led fighter-bombers to 15 vehicles and three tanks hidden in some woods near Hilders. As the P-47s began their attack an American column was heading right toward the waiting Germans, but by the time the Americans would have been in range, the fighter-bombers had turned the German position into a raging inferno. As Goodermote left the scene he was gratified to see the column of Sherman tanks safely rumbling past the shattered remains of the German position and on toward their objective.

A convoy of vehicles and personnel of the 10th PRG crosses the Rhine River at Mainz on 1 April 1945. (credit: Robert Anderson)

When his first Mustang, named *Miss Minookie*, was lost in combat while being flown by another pilot, Captain Dale Goodermote received this new F-6D, coded 5M✪A, s/n 44-14715. This aircraft, also named *Miss Minookie* was assigned to Goodermote in the Spring of 1945. *(credit: Stewart Wilson)*

landing. Since US troops had been seen in the immediate area, Lieutenant Shively did not strafe the Bf 109 in case of inflicting "friendly fire."

On 4 April, the 12th TRS enjoyed its greatest day to date in terms of aerial victories with a total of four; Lieutenant Leo Elliott accounted for 1.5 of the total. Lieutenant Elliott reported his day as follows: *"We were halfway through our reconnaissance when I spotted a Ju 88 bomber dead ahead and below us. That target was too good to pass up so with my wingman, Lt. Dan Cartago, following me, I dived on the plane, fired, and set his left engine on fire. I was going to overshoot him so I peeled off to the right and my wingman finished him off, shooting at him until he hit the ground. As I peeled off I noticed a Ju 87 off to the right. All my guns but one were jammed, but I used that, following him to the deck. He was going so slow I started to overshoot just as we came to a high-tension wire. I was right above him then and couldn't pull up enough to clear the wire, so I squeezed under it. When I looked back I saw that the German, trying to get away from me, had flown too low and crashed into the ground."*

Lieutenant "Lee" Larson. The section was checking railroads when it encountered a Ju 188 near Wittenburg. Captain East made the first pass, and fired three bursts at the bomber, hitting the fuselage and left engine, which burst into flames. Lieutenant Larson then hit the German aircraft from the right side and his gunfire set the right engine ablaze. As Larson pulled up he saw the bomber slide off into a gentle dive and explode at 1,500 ft. About an hour later the section spotted a Fw 190 flying at about 2,000 ft, 15 miles south of Leipzig, and East attacked from six o'clock. He opened fire from about 100 yds and his machine guns blew the Fw 190 apart, and apparently killed the pilot because the enemy aircraft went into a slow roll, dived to the ground, and exploded on impact.

When weather forced Lieutenant Bob Shively to abort his mission, he compensated for a blank reconnaissance report by scoring an economical victory over a Bf 109. The encounter took place in the vicinity of Germerade when Shively saw the enemy aircraft flying east at deck level. He made a tight diving turn to the right and leveled out right on the Bf 109's tail, but before he could open fire, the German saw him, panicked and bellied his aircraft in for a crash-

Lieutenant Leo Elliott poses by his F-6D *Tampa Joe*, ZM✪F, s/n 44-14775. The artwork on his aircraft was another of the "masterpieces" painted by Lloyd Hoobery. Elliott was a native of Tampa, Florida and the "Joe" was after a friend serving in the 79th Infantry Division. *(credit: Leo Elliott)*

Next to fall was a Bf 109 which Captain Bill Winberry encountered near Gotha and shot down in a brief encounter. The fourth kill of the day was a Fieseler Storch that was shared by Lts. Bob Bruce and Bob "Hotshot" Gardner. Their combined firepower made quick work of the fragile liaison aircraft, which disintegrated when hit and tumbled to earth and exploded.

Missions of 5 April added more German aircraft to the 10th PRG's scoreboard when its pilots destroyed three more in aerial combat and one on the ground. Lts. Mingo Logothetis and John "Red" Ellis of the 12th TRS encountered a mixed flight of three Bf 109s and three Fw 190s near Gotha and in the ensuing melee each of them destroyed an Fw 190. Lieutenant Logothetis managed to damage the remaining Fw 190 before breaking off to escort Ellis – whose Mustang had been damaged in the dogfight – back to base. The section made it to within two of miles of the base when Ellis' engine failed and he was forced to jump. He landed safely and returned by motor transport later in the day.

The destruction of the *Luftwaffe* continued when Lts. Norbert Kirkpatrick and Stewart Wilson of the 15th TRS encountered a Stuka near Munchberg. The section was checking movement on the *autobahn* when Kirkpatrick spotted the enemy aircraft flying northward at 1,000 ft. Kirkpatrick pushed his Mustang into a dive and closed to 200 yds, opened fire, and then watched as the Stuka mushed out of its flight path and crashed to earth.

Lt. Bob Gardner's F-6C *Hotshot Charlie*, ZM✪U, s/n 43-25162. The artwork was created by Lloyd Hoobery and the aircraft name came from Lt. Gardner's marked resemblance to Hotshot Charlie of the "Terry and the Pirates" comic strip, and also as a result of his speedy landings! (*credit: William Davenport*)

Numerous targets were also detected on the ground by pilots of the 15th TRS and Lts. Henry Lacey, Haylon Wood, and Bob Shively led fighter-bombers to them. Lieutenant Lacey began the assault with an attack on two military trains, and Wood found another loaded with trucks and armor, all of which were clobbered by the Thunderbolts. Bob Shively led another squadron of P-47s to 25 aircraft, mostly Bf 109s, parked in some woods and personally destroyed one of them during the strike. Before leaving the scene, Shively witnessed the destruction of three more Bf 109s by the P-47s.

Most of the 31st PS personnel were preparing to move to Ober-Olm during the day, but Captain Harold Leuth had an urgent mission to take care of first. His assignment was to photograph 150 miles of the *autobahn*, stretching from Eisenach to Dresden. His mission was a complete success and the photos were rushed to the Third Army to use in its preparations for a drive toward Czechoslovakia.

Seventeen sections of aircraft of the 15th TRS flew a variety of missions on 7 April 1945, and its pilots filed

reports pertaining to German rail activity, troop movements, and a skirmish in progress. Lieutenant Al Frick led Thunderbolts to a cluster of six tanks and 50 trucks near Holtzhalloben and witnessed the punishing attack administered to the hapless German troops and vehicles on the ground. Near Effelder Lieutenant Norbert Kirkpatrick kept a close eye on a tank battle between 12 US and 12 German tanks to see if reinforcements were required. Numerous vehicles were seen burning near the American tanks and Kirkpatrick alerted nearby Thunderbolts of the battle in progress.

As the German line of defense continued to shrink, the *Luftwaffe* tried to provide air cover for its friends on the ground by intercepting the snooping tactical reconnaissance sections. This was especially true for the team of Mingo Logothetis and John Ellis during their mission of 7 April. They encountered Fw 190s twice during their mission to the Darmstadt area and were victorious on both occasions. The first engagement took

Before and after. Lieutenant John Ellis and his F-6C (left) seen prior to his mission of 5 April 1945, and the wreckage of the aircraft (right) after its engine failed on the trip back to base. (*credit: John R. Ellis*)

Clyde East's *Lil Margaret* undergoing maintenance at Trier, Germany. (*credit: Clyde B. East*)

place at 18.50 hrs when they spotted three Fw 190s in formation and scored a shared victory over one of them. Ten minutes later the section found another Fw 190 and watched it crash and explode after they had laced the fuselage and canopy with their combined firepower.

The 10th PRG had an exceptional day on 8 April. The Group turned in a volume of reconnaissance reports to the Third Army, and claimed ten enemy aircraft in the process.

Eight of the aerial victories were claimed by the 15th TRS, and the first kill of the day was an Fw 190 downed by Lieutenant Norborne Thomas 20 miles southeast of Regensburg. The encounter was a brief one. After receiving the report of the enemy fighter from his wingman, Lieutenant Bob Shively, Thomas broke to the right, followed the diving enemy aircraft down to about 3,000 ft and pulled in behind it. Thomas opened fire at a range of 200 yds and closed to 50 yds, observing hits all over the fuselage. As white smoke began to emit from the enemy aircraft's cockpit, it slid from its path and began to glide to the left. As the Fw 190 fell into its fatal dive, Shively hit it with one final burst and he and Thomas watched as it hit the ground and came apart.

As Norbert Thomas's victim crashed to earth, two other engagements were taking place. While flying near Juterburg, Captain John Hoefker spotted a He 111 bomber and shot it down for victory number 9.5. At just about the same time, Captain Clyde East and Lieutenant "Lee" Larson were raising havoc with a flight of three Ju 87s near Dresden. East attacked the one on the left and Larson took the one on the right. East opened fire from 200 yds and saw white smoke pour back from the stricken Stuka prior to it going into a split-S and crashing to earth. Larson pulled in from behind his target and observed it do a wingover and dive into the ground after he had ripped its fuselage and engine apart with a long burst from his machine guns. The third Stuka began circling the wreckage of one of the downed German aircraft and Captain East quickly shot it down. A few seconds later the section spotted a He 111 circling a wrecked aircraft

and attacked. East struck from the left and Larson from the right and the Heinkel fell to earth, bounced, hit the ground again, broke apart, and burned. About an hour later, when the section was in vicinity of Riesa, Captain East encountered a Si 104 transport aircraft and shot it down with one long burst. The enemy aircraft began to fall apart immediately after being hit by East's concentrated burst of gunfire. As its fuselage broke in half and its wings folded, the four-man crew tried to jump, but a spinning wing killed two of them outright and a third crew member died after his parachute opened improperly. The remaining German parachuted safely. With these 3.5 victories Clyde East raised his total to 12 and passed Captain John Hoefker as the 10th PRG's top Ace.

In the last air battle of the day Lieutenant Charles "Chuck" Rowland outfought an Fw 190 that had bounced his section as it headed back to base. The Fw 190 opened fire on Rowland at a range of approximately 700 yards and missed. After failing in his attack the German pilot tried to escape by making a 180-degree turn, but his maneuver did not work. Rowland quickly latched onto the enemy aircraft's tail and shot it down with a well-placed burst from 100 yds. His gunfire smashed the canopy and with a dead man at the controls, the Fw 190 slid off into a turn and crashed at the edge of a field.

The 10th PRG's other aerial victories of 8 April were credited to the 12th TRS. The Squadron's first kill of the day was an Fw 190 which Lieutenant Henry Ermatinger downed near Hof at 08.00 hrs and its second was claimed at

The He 111 bomber shot down by Captain Clyde East and Lieutenant "Lee" Larson on 8 April 1945. (*credit: Clyde B. East*)

Lt. Charles "Chuck" Rowland of the 15th TRS posing with an Fw 190 captured at Fürth on 8 May 1945. *(credit: Charles Rowland)*

chased him over the treetops for over 20 miles. We damaged him alright, but weren't doing too much good, and as we were finishing our route when we were attacked we were pretty low on gas, so we finally gave it up and came on home."

The Squadron's remaining victories of the day were by Lts. John Ellis and Mingo Logothetis. The section was headed east near Bayreuth at 3,500 ft when two Fw 190s approached it from six o'clock. The section broke before the German fighters were within firing range and made a 180-degree turn for a head-on pass at the enemy aircraft. Seeing the Mustangs coming at them, the Fw 190s turned away and in doing so, presented themselves as easy targets. Logothetis and Ellis then selected their respective victims and quickly shot them out of the sky. One of the Germans was able to escape his flaming ship by parachute.

The numerous aerial victories during the month of April brought about a great feeling of pride and *esprit de corps* within the 10th PRG, but that feeling was not universal. By now reports of these kills had reached Headquarters, XIX Tactical Air Command and General O.P. Weyland reacted swiftly. In the opinion of General Weyland and his staff, these aerial combats jeopardized the primary mission of reconnaissance and were to be stopped immediately. His directive stated that no reconnaissance pilot under his command would fire at any German aircraft unless it was in the process of attacking the reconnaissance flight or friendly forces on the ground. (His ire was probably increased by the fact that one transport and two liaison aircraft were included in the victory totals.) This edict was not popular among

19.00 hrs by Lieutenant John "Dusty" Rhodes near Gotha. In the second encounter, Rhodes' section was bounced by a Bf 109 flown by a poor marksman. After making its firing pass and missing, the Bf 109 attempted to get away, but to no avail. Forty-five seconds later it spiraled to earth and crashed after receiving a punishing barrage from Lieutenant Rhodes' guns.

The 12th TRS continued its victorious ways on 9 April with four more kills. Two of them were claimed by the team of Bill Davenport and Ron Ricci and the details were outlined in Davenport's report: *"It was the first mission that I was leading and suddenly these three 190s came in at us from out of the sun. We didn't see them until they were firing, but fortunately they overshot us and we were on their tails before they knew it. From then on it was duck soup.*

"Two were line abreast, the third higher and in front of the other two. I told Lt. Ricci to take the one on the left and I'd take the one on the right. My first burst scored hits all over the 190, and he went to pieces, rolled over on his back and just seemed to slip right into the ground. My wingman got his too, and the pilot bailed out. Then we joined up on the third, who hit the deck, and we

Lieutenant Bill Davenport and crew chief S/Sgt. Ernie Weiss pose with their F-6C *Bama Bell*, named after Davenport's home state of Alabama. This Mustang was coded ZM◒L I (bar), s/n unknown. At a later date, artist Lloyd Hoobery added a Vargas girl-style painting behind the name, and changed the spelling of *"Bell"* to *"Belle"*. *(credit: William Davenport)*

most tactical reconnaissance pilots and Captain Clyde East noted in his diary: "*Things did not change appreciably during the next few days. We found the restrictions more mental than physical. Outside the fact that non-combat type aircraft were excluded from attack, business went on about the same as usual.*"

General Weyland, however, meant what he said and as we will see later, some of the 10th PRG's pilots were to suffer for transgressing against his orders.

The 15th TRS flew 19 missions on 9 April and its pilots directed devastating assaults upon rail and road traffic. Two of the Squadron's missions were flown by Captain Clyde East and on each occasion he found tempting targets for the fighter-bombers. On his first mission

5M✪T of the 15th TRS. This is the former *Peachy's Delight* flown by "Bud" Schonard as 5M✪C. After Schonard's departure, this aircraft became the favorite mount of Lieutenant Howard Nichols. Note the aircraft has now been fitted with a fin strake and bears unfinished group and squadron markings on its nose and tail. (*credit: Stewart Wilson*)

East led P-47s to a train unloading trucks and armor at a railroad siding, destroyed four trucks himself, and then hung around to watch the Thunderbolts dispose of the remainder. On his next mission he led fighter-bombers to a column of 200 vehicles he had found at Erfurt and destroyed three of them before stepping aside to let the P-47s finish the job.

Ground fog and low-hanging clouds covered most of the Group's assigned target areas on 10 April but these weather conditions did not eliminate aerial encounters for pilots of the 15th TRS. Near Leipzig, two enemy aircraft, an Fw 190 and a Bf 109, made the mistake of attacking Lts. Wayne Patrick and Richard McFadden. Again, poor gunnery by German pilots allowed Patrick and McFadden to escape the attack and soon thereafter the hunters became the hunted. Both enemy aircraft were hit repeatedly by the section's gunfire, but due to the undercast, the American pilots did not see them crash. However, each pilot was credited with a probable. In other action, Lieutenant Henry Lacey encountered an overzealous Bf 110 and sent it crashing into a field near Torgau and Captain John Hoefker topped off the day with a big reconnaissance report and another kill. Hoefker recalled his final victory with this description: "*Lt. Charles White and I were patrolling the German rail system near Hof when I spotted an Fw 190 loafing along under us. I told Lt. White to take him,*

An Fw 190 crashes to earth on 10 April 1945 having just been shot down by Captain John Hoefker. This was Hoefker's last of 10.5 victories. (*credit: John H. Hoefker*)

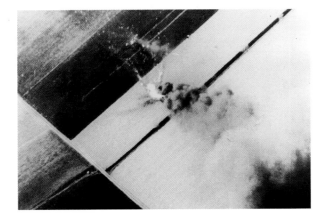

but while we were making our turn, White lost sight of the enemy aircraft. I realized Lt. White had lost him, and not wanting the 190 to get away, I attacked and hit him with a concentrated burst. The 190 burst into flames, dived into the ground, and exploded."

This was victory number 10.5 for Captain Hoefker and it turned out to be his last of the war.

The leash on the Third Army was finally released on 11 April 1945 and it burst forth toward the east and at the same time extended its southern flank to Bayreuth in order to maintain its contact with the Seventh Army. Before the day was out, the 4th Armored Division had pushed 40 miles and had captured or encircled several towns, including Jena, Weimar, and the infamous Buchenwald concentration camp. The advance continued on 12 April and by late afternoon of 14 April, the Third Army had pushed to with 20 miles of Leipzig, 35 miles from Dresden, and 10 miles from the Czechoslovakian border, only to have the leash put back on it by General Eisenhower.

Radio problems and haze affected the missions flown by the 15th TRS on 11 April, but its pilots still managed to produce some excellent results. Lieutenant Chuck Rowland led fighter-bombers to three separate targets near Saalfeld; a concentration of 30 motor vehicles; a marshaling yard crowded with boxcars, flatcars and locomotives with steam up; and a column of 150 troops and their support vehicles. Lieutenant Henry Lacey led a squadron of P-47s to 25 large vehicles towing trailers and watched them bomb and strafe the convoy. When the attack was completed the road was blocked with the burning hulks of the entire convoy. A little later in the day Lieutenant John Miefert led P-47s to eight 88 mm anti-tank guns that were holding up the advance of an American tank column and saw the guns destroyed by a number of direct bomb strikes.

The weather worsened on 13 April and forced many tactical reconnaissance pilots to abort their primary missions. In the cases of the pilots that were able to continue, however, the action was often hot and heavy. Five miles south of Hof, two Bf 109s sneaked in on Clyde East and Bill Meikle from out of the sun while they were concentrating on another flight of 20 Bf 109s flying west at 6,000 ft. Captain East's Mustang was hit four times with one of the shells piercing his right fuel tank. Nevertheless, East turned into the Bf 109 that had fired at him, jettisoned his wing tanks, climbed, and moved in for the kill. After positioning himself on the Bf 109's tail, East opened fire and observed hits on its fuselage and left wing, after which the enemy aircraft broke to the right and headed down trailing black smoke and crash-landed. It was victory number 13.

The heavy tactical reconnaissance activity continued on 15 April and resulted in more punishment for Germans on the ground and in the air. The first dogfight of the day occurred when a Bf 109 attacked Lts. Bill Davenport and Ron Ricci near Eger. The enemy aircraft came in at them from nine o'clock, fired, and missed. The section quickly maneuvered for attack and Davenport took the first crack at the enemy aircraft but his gunfire went wide of the target. At this point Ricci was in firing position and scored numerous hits on the Bf 109's engine, fuselage, and wings. As the enemy aircraft's engine then burst into flame Lieutenant Ricci opened fire again and the German pilot took to his parachute.

The 15th TRS was busy on 15 April and the Squadron scribe recounted the activity: *"Eighteen missions were completed. Weather and lack of activity limited observations on some flights, but on others excellent work was done in cooperation with the fighter-bombers. (Lt. Wayne) Patrick led fighter-bombers to two military trains and one engine. One of the new pilots, Lt. (Harry S.) Utley, scored his first victory when a Me-Bf 109 made a steep diving pass at his section. Utley chased the Bf 109 and shot it down. Lt. Goodermote and his wingman led fighter-bombers to 300-plus MT (motor transports) and some horse-drawn carts moving south in the vicinity of Freiburg. An estimated 150 of the concentration were destroyed. (Lt.*

Chuck) Rowland continued the good work, taking fighter-bombers to a point near Rozwein where they hammered a concentration of 40 plus MT, 10-plus medium tanks, and 15 horse-drawn carts including five artillery pieces with bombs, rockets and hard-hitting 50s. The attack resulted in the destruction of half the tanks, trucks, and carts. (Lt. Henry) Lacey picked up 20-plus MT and a prime mover towing two 88s for the P-47s. On his second mission of the day Lt. Patrick found another military train. (Lt. Charles) White brought the day to a close by leading fighter-bombers to ten halftracks and five trucks near Chemnitz."

Action continued to be plentiful for the 15th TRS on 16 April and its pilots again saw to the destruction of German forces in the air and on the ground. Another aerial victory was claimed when a flight of three Bf 109s

ABOVE: After his return from the mission of 13 April 1945 during which he scored his 13th and final victory, Captain East was photographed by the Public Relations Officer. (*credit: Clyde B. East*)

BELOW: Captain East's F-6D in its final markings. Note that *Lil Margaret* is now applied in large red "Old English" lettering under the exhaust stacks and the aircraft displays its pilot's full score of 13 kills. (*credit: Clyde B. East*)

Lt. Harry S. Utley of the 15th TRS poses with Lt. Brown of the 354th FG on Major L.K. Brueland's Mustang at Erfurt. Both men were from Henderson, Kentucky. (credit: Harry S. Utley)

with a solitary Fw 190 as top cover attempted to intercept Lts. Al Frick and Harry Utley. The enemy aircraft tried to attack the section from the four o'clock position, but Frick and Utley saw them coming and pulled up abruptly. As the Bf 109s passed under them each pilot chose his target, closed in for the kill, and shot it down.

Lieutenant Haylon Wood added to the retreating *Wehrmacht's* woes by finding a number of rail and highway targets and leading the fighter-bombers to the attack. In another situation Lts. Ed Goval and Merlin Reed found themselves in the unusual position of having to stop an attack by three P-47s of the 405th Fighter Squadron on American forces north of Plauen. They were able to stop the attack by boxing in one of the Thunderbolts and escorting him out of the area. Apparently the two other Thunderbolt pilots must have "gotten the message" from watching this maneuver and broke off their attack. After diverting the P-47s, Goval and Reed determined that the troops below had not laid out their identifying colors-of-the-day panels, and notified the controller so corrections could be made.

The 16th of April was also another day of movement and the forward elements of the 15th TRS headed for their new base at Erfurt. The rear echelon continued to operate from Ober-Olm until 18 April and the first-light missions were launched there and ended at Erfurt. The remainder of the aircraft were brought to Erfurt during the day and a C-47 shuttled back and forth to bring the remaining personnel and light equipment. The Squadron diary contains these comments about the move: "*It was an amusing and incredible sight that greeted the rear echelon when they alighted from the plane. Scrounging expeditions had netted a number of pleasure cars and motorcycles. The perimeter track looked like Riverside Drive on a busy day. German motorcycles and automobiles made a steady stream of traffic around the field. To add color to the scene a number of the men wore odds and ends of German uniforms picked up in storerooms and warehouses. It was more like Hollywood than war.*"

On 17 April, the Third Army received orders to halt its eastward drive and turn south toward Munich. This drastic change of direction called for extensive mapping of the southern areas of Germany and the "Redoubt Area," located in Bavaria between Berchtesgaden and Salzburg, Austria. It was believed that Hitler had planned for a strong last-ditch stand of Nazi Germany here, and it would be the Third Army's job to wreck it. In order to assist in the Third Army preparations for this campaign, the 31st PS photographed several thousand square miles of southern Germany in one week, beginning on 17 April. The job was not without opposition and German fighters were up daily in an attempt to disrupt these missions. Most of the 31st pilots were able to evade attacks from both German jet and piston-engine fighters, but not all. On 20 April Lieutenant D.C. Davis was over Nuremberg when he was jumped by a formation of 22 Bf 109s. Davis spotted the swarm of enemy aircraft as they approached and climbed to evade them, but an unseen Bf 109 sneaked in and crippled his right engine. After being hit, Davis' F-5 fell off into a steep dive trailing smoke and coolant. His assailant must have thought Davis was a confirmed kill and did not follow the diving F-5. After safely evading the

This F-6D of the 15th TRS crash-landed at Y-84 Giessen, Germany before its ground crew had time to paint squadron and group markings on its nose and tail. (credit: Donald Stonestrom via Jim Crow)

ABOVE: B Flight of the 15th TRS. Standing left to right: Henry Lacey, "Lee" Larson, Clyde East, Merlin Reed, Fairfield Goodale, Robert Ober. On the wing, from left to right: Wayne Patrick, Charles Johnson, Phillip Hunt. (*credit: William N. Hess*)

RIGHT: Personnel of the 12th TRS show off captured Nazi flags and banners found at Fürth. (*credit: E. L. Bishop*)

The 162nd TRS flight line at Fürth. Note the Mustangs are still wearing their old unit markings – a yellow nose band with a black border at the rear and a yellow spinner. (*credit: William I. Williams*)

pronged attacked to finish the job. Its northern thrust was toward eastern Germany, its eastward push was toward Czechoslovakia, and its southern spearhead headed into the Austrian Alps. Attacking on a 140-mile front, Third Army units met fierce opposition, but poor road and rough terrain were its main obstacles. The final collapse of the *Wehrmacht* began on 2 May, when the commander-in-chief of all German forces in Italy surrendered, and gathered momentum on 3 and 4 May when German troops in Holland, north-west Germany, Denmark, and the Friesian Island chain surrendered.

During these last few days of hostilities the 10th's tactical reconnaissance pilots took the opportunity to get in a few last punches at its faltering foe and scored in the air and on the ground. On 3 May Lts. Henry Lacey and Wayne Patrick of the 15th TRS were contacted by a liaison pilot who stated that a four man *Panzerfaust* and machine gun crew was holding up the advance of an American column and asked for their assistance. Lacey and Patrick quickly located the German position and killed all four of its team in a strafing attack. On the following day F/O Robert Roper and Lieutenant Glen Gremillion of the 162nd TRS bounced a "cream colored" Ju 88 eight miles north-east of Linz, Austria and Gremillion destroyed it without firing a shot. His encounter report stated: "*On 4 May while running a visual recce in the Linz area I spotted a twin-engined aircraft flying at two o'clock at about 1,000 feet. I was at 10,000 feet and turned and lost a little altitude to identify the plane. As I came closer I recognized it as a Ju 88. It had black crosses on the wings and a swastika on the tail. Apparently the Ju 88 identified me as the enemy because he cut his switches and attempted to belly-land. He crashed in an open field, completely destroying his aircraft, and without a doubt killing the whole crew. The Ju 88 burned for only a short time, and I did not fire at him. I took pictures of the crash. I claim 1 Ju 88 destroyed.*"

On 5 May Patton's 16th Armored Division liberated Pilsen, Czechoslovakia, home of the famous beer, and requisitioned huge quantities of the golden beverage for the celebration. News of the final collapse came on 6 May when word came down that Admiral Dönitz, as leader of the Nazi Government, was negotiating the final surrender and now all there was to do was wait.

The final day of the war, 8 May 1945, was to become one of the most incredible days in the 10th PRG's operational history. Its tactical reconnaissance pilots spent most of the day as aerial cowboys rounding up surrendering German aircraft and escorting them to Fürth. Lts. Bill Brackett and Floyd Lofland escorted an Arado Ar 96 training aircraft to Ronecken airfield while the German in the back seat of the enemy aircraft waved a white handkerchief. Lts. Dick McFadden and Bob Shively had a field day when they met three Fw 190s, three Bf 109s, a Ju 88, and a Ju 188. They led one of the Bf 109s to a small field where they and the Fw 190 landed. After overseeing the surrender of the pilot, Fw. Herbert Showranek, and his passenger who had ridden in the radio compartment, McFadden and Shively turned the prisoners over to an Engineer unit and then took off and returned to escort the rest of its German formation into captivity. Next they shepherded one of the Fw 190s and the two bombers to R-43 and after seeing them surrender, escorted the remaining four enemy aircraft to Fürth.

As Lts. Bob Jeffrey and Julian Biniewski escorted a Bf 109 to Fürth, it broke into the section and made a pass at Jeffrey. An enraged Jeffrey evaded the attack and then bore in on his assailant and scored hits with a deflection shot. As he broke off Lieutenant Biniewski closed and shot the Bf 109 down with two long bursts.

Lt. Dick McFadden's Mustang parked next to one of the Fw 190s that he and Lt. Bob Shively captured on 8 May 1945. (*credit: Richard McFadden*)

During the 15th's last mission of the day, Lts. "Lee" Larson and George Schroeder had a similar experience while trying to escort two Fw 190s to the base. As the section approached the Fw 190s, the enemy aircraft reacted in an aggressive manner and a brief dogfight ensued. Lieutenant Schroeder followed one of the Fw 190s to the deck and pursued it until it smashed into some trees, and Larson fastened himself on the tail of the other enemy aircraft. This Focke-Wulf dived to 500 ft, made a tight turn to the left – too tight – snapped into a spin and crashed. The only shots fired were those by the 190s in their first and only offensive action of the encounter. Schroeder's Mustang received a single hit in its left wing.

The 162nd Tactical Reconnaissance Squadron's historian recorded the day and his squadron's part in it: "*Tuesday, May 8, 1945 was by all means the strangest day in nearly 17 months. The whole German Air Force went out to return to its old bases and give up to the Yanks, with nearly 20 planes and 30 people landing at R-28 alone, all herded in by pilots from the 12th, 15th, or 162nd, who found them willing prisoners in most cases. The first, an Me-Bf 109 was forced in by Lt. Stanley Newman and Lt. Manuel Geiger about noon. From then on Bf 109s and Stukas drifted in incessantly, wagging their wings, and swerving off the runway after they were down. There must have been 1,000 men on the field, waiting to pick up pistols and get a look at these planes. Our second capture was made by Lt. Ray Conley and Captain Elvin Young, a 190; the third by Lts. Geiger and Stanley Newman, a Siebel 104, and the last, another 190 by Lts. George Alm and Frank Seely. This last one was a recalcitrant who first made a fast break which was cut off by a faster pursuit and a few rounds along the German's fuselage; but then, coming in, he pulled up his gear on the runway and settled there, making it necessary for Lt. Alm to wait around in the dark with a low gas tank before the runway was clear. In all this we netted four planes and*

Lieutenant Manuel Geiger's F-6C *Miss Ann* at Fürth. The full code and serial number of this aircraft are unknown. (*credit: Stanley Newman*)

about a dozen prisoners for the 162nd. Two of the planes, a Bf 109 and a 190, will be turned over to Engineering for keepsakes.

"*There were three other noteworthy missions, one routine and two special. The first, with Lt. Manuel Geiger and Lt. Stanley Newman (who flew three missions on the 8th) shooting down two Fw 190s in Czechoslovakia, each claiming one.*"

The section was jumped by the Fw 190s six miles south-east of Bischofteinitz. The section quickly broke into the Focke-Wulfs, which immediately headed for the deck. Lieutenant Newman and Lieutenant Geiger followed their respective Fw 190s down, and the enemy aircraft began rolling back and forth and reversing their turns. Newman fired a four-second burst, observed hits all over the Focke-Wulf's tail section and watched as the enemy aircraft continued on down and crash-landed. While this encounter was taking place Lieutenant Geiger bested the second Fw 190 and sent it down. Both downed aircraft were photographed for confirmation.

In regard to the two special missions the 162nd diary stated: "*The two special missions were flown on the 7th over the POW camps at Lienz, Spital, Klagenfurt, Wolfsburg, and Liebnitz. Lts. Conrad Wright and John Goodrich flew the first and Goodrich was forced to land on an enemy airfield near Graz after his engine was hit by flak. (After he landed at Graz the Germans took away his .45 pistol, but then decided they were doing it all wrong, and gave him back his own weapon as well as theirs, and he took over. All of them took off to the nearest American unit, and Goodrich presented the station complement to be interned. He then returned to Fürth on May 13th.) The second mission, which was flown by Lts. Russell Scara and Ronald Olson, was uneventful and they returned with excellent photos of the camps.*"

In the spirit of the occasion the pilots of the 12th TRS escorted in their fair share of the surrendering *Luftwaffe* too. Lts. Dale Shimon and E. J. O'Brien forced an Fw 190 D to land at

One of the Fw 190s captured by Lts. McFadden and Shively. The German pilot in the cockpit waits to be taken prisoner, 8 May 1945. (*credit: Richard McFadden*)

Linz, Lt. Don Lynch forced another to land at R-28 and Lts. Ed Kenny and Robert Marple forced a third Fw 190 into a belly landing at R-28. The highlight of the day, however, was the mission flown by Lt. Robert C. Little. As he and his wingman, Lt. Wallace Mitchell, were patrolling the River Danube, the section was bounced by a flight of five Fw 190s. After successfully evading the attack, Lt. Little fell in behind the flight of enemy aircraft and sent one of them down in flames. Bob Little's victory was scored at 20.00 hrs on 8 May 1945, making it was the last aerial victory scored in the European Theater of Operations.

Four hours after Lt. Little's victory it was all over in Europe and the 10th Photo Reconnaissance Group settled into its duties as part of the Army of Occupation. In its fourteen months of combat operations the Group established and maintained a record of excellence second to none, and certainly earned its slogan of "First on D-Day – Last on VE Day."

ABOVE: Lieutenant Don Lynch of the 12th TRS escorts a surrendering Fw 190 into Fürth, 8 May 1945. (*credit: Don Lynch*)

RIGHT: Lieutenant Robert C. Little of the 12th TRS scored the last aerial "kill" of the war in Europe in ZM✪G, s/n 42-103209 at 20.00 hrs, 8 May 1945.

LEFT: An interesting photograph of "Lee" Larson's 5M✪M. Note the drop tank which has been converted into a "dicing" camera mounted under the left wing. The aircraft is sporting six crosses indicating Lieutenant Larson's victory tally and a bare metal spinner. (*credit: Raymond Gaudette*)

BELOW: Bob Hope and Jerry Cologna are all set to christen Lloyd Hoobery's artwork on Lieutenant Ed Kenny's *Shovelnose and Handlebar*. This 12th TRS aircraft was coded ZM✪E, s/n 42-103615. It was also decorated with a Vargas girl under the canopy opening, compliments of the previous pilot, Lieutenant Robert Hanson. (*credit: Douglas Gibson via Jim Crow*)

HEADQUARTERS
XIX TACTICAL AIR COMMAND

APO 141, U S Army,
9 May 1945.

GENERAL ORDERS)
:
NUMBER .....34)

TO THE OFFICERS AND MEN

OF THE

XIX TACTICAL AIR COMMAND

At one minute past midnight this morning the German enemy's career of crime ended in unconditional surrender to Allied arms, the mightiest concentration of air, land and sea power ever assembled to curb and smash an aggressor nation.

To each of you, this is a personal victory, for the efforts of every officer and man have contributed to the effectiveness of the XIX Tactical Air Command - Third US Army team, which has carried air-ground cooperation to new heights of combat efficiency and beaten the enemy at every turn.

Through the fortunes of war and the aggressiveness of our great comrade-at-arms, the Third Army, this Command has been continually in the forefront of the battle, from Normandy to the heart of the enemy's homeland and on across the borders of Austria and Czechoslovakia. For more than nine months we have had the Hun on the run, until at last he could run no farther. The day of victory finds us rounding up the last scattered remnants of the beaten foe and escorting his once-warlike pilots to our bases in abject surrender.

Upon the successful conclusion of our mission, I want to express my heartfelt admiration and appreciation for all that each of you has done to make possible this victory. Your prowess and devotion are a credit to our country -- and there is no higher praise.

O. P. WEYLAND,
Major General, USA,
Commanding.

DISTRIBUTION "C"

APPENDICES

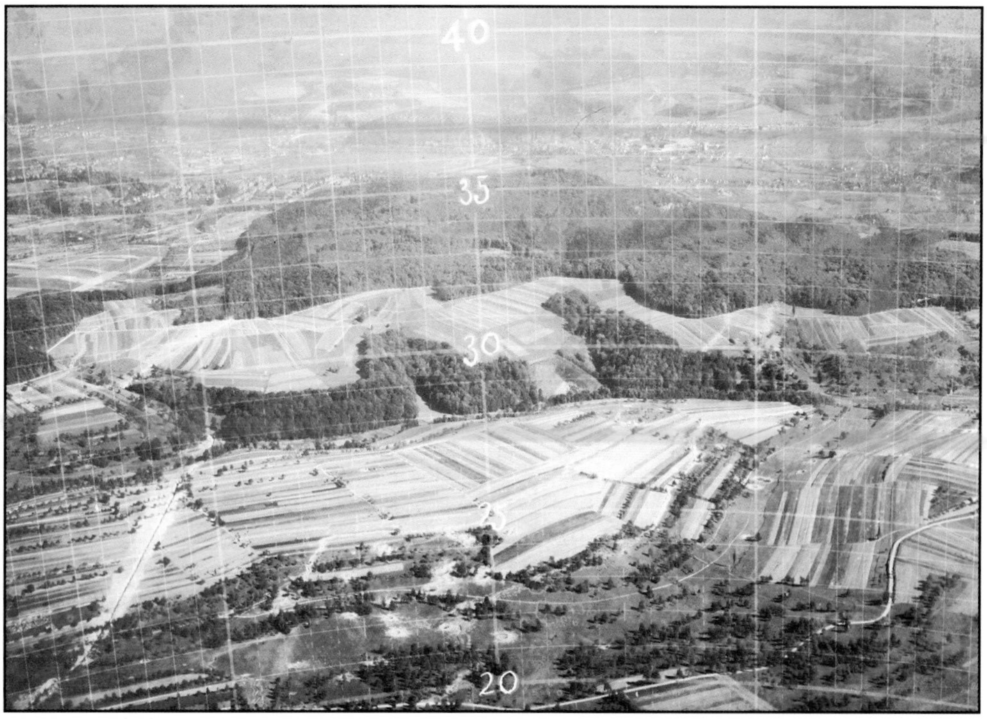

APPENDICES

APPENDIX ONE

AIRCRAFT AND TACTICS OF THE 10TH PHOTO RECONNAISSANCE GROUP

TAC R

Tactical Reconnaissance pilots in the 10th PRG operated the photo version of the P-51 Mustang which was designated the F-6. The comparative F-6 designation to the fighter version was as follows:

F-6B – P-51A   F-6C – P-51B/C
F-6D – P-51D   F-6K – P-51K

The basic difference between the fighter and the reconnaissance version was the installation of cameras in the fuselage section. Unlike the photo version of the P-38 which carried no guns, the TAC R pilot retained the full four or six-gun armament carried by fighter pilots and, although he was ordered to avoid combat whenever possible, could defend himself against enemy aircraft.

For vertical photography the F-6 normally carried the K-22 camera with a 12-in. cone, which could produce detailed photos from an altitude of 6,000 ft, or the K-17 with a 6-in. cone which was used for altitudes of 3,500 ft. The K-17 was later replaced with a 6-in. version of the K-22 which provided a two-second rewind cycle for overlap coverage at low altitude.

For missions which required oblique photography, the F-6 carried either the K-24 camera which had a 7-in. or 14 in cone or a K-22 with the 12-in. cone. The K-24 was utilized for low altitude oblique coverage of railway tunnels, cuts, and bridges. These photographs were very useful in briefing fighter-bomber pilots for attacking such facilities.

For taking Merton Gridded Oblique Photos the K-22 camera was used. These photos were generally taken at altitudes ranging from 2,500-4,000 ft and from an angle of 12-17 degrees. These gridded photographs were valuable to both artillery commanders and field commanders in planning barrages and assaults.

LEFT: Early F-6B/C aircraft converted from P-51Bs often saw their vertical photographs ruined due to the fact that the lens became mud-covered during take-offs.
(credit: James Collins)

LEFT: The 15th TRS' experienced photo officer, Captain Chris Fette, was quick to solve the mud problem by developing a hinged lens cover for the Mustang's vertical camera and as a result pilots returned from missions with excellent photographs.
(Mrs. Alma Fette)

LEFT: This simple modification, devised by Captain Fette, insured a clean, unobstructed lens for the rest of the war.
(credit: Air Force Museum)

TAC R Missions and Tactics

The normal TAC R mission consisted of a two-aircraft flight called a section with the more experienced pilot acting as section leader. The leader or #1 pilot was responsible for navigation and for observing or photographing the target zone, while it was the #2 man's responsibility to provide protection against air attack and warning against *flak*. The #2 man always flew approximately 200 yds to the immediate flank of the leader and down sun from him so that #1's tail was always covered toward the sun, from where the German attacks generally took place.

For visual recce missions they usually flew between 3,500 and 6,000 ft, although TAC R photo missions sometimes ran higher. The visual recce was limited to a maximum of 6,000 ft because beyond that the ground cannot be discerned in sufficient detail. Many times it was necessary to go below 3,500 ft to make specific observation, such as what a particular train was carrying as its load, etc.

Tactical reconnaissance is generally broken down into the following types of missions:

A: Area Search

To provide the Commanding General of an army area with immediate information on movement and disposition of troops within its boundaries and along its front, and the area consisted of all territory within the Army boundaries to a depth of approximately 100 miles beyond its front line. Because the area was so large it was usually sub-divided into smaller areas of 650 square miles, and an area of this size could be completely covered by one section in an hour. Before the section took off on this type of mission they were thoroughly briefed on the situation by an Army Ground Liaison Officer and were given a few specific points to check in addition to the area coverage.

B: Route Recce

This type of mission was normally a visual recce of rail lines and highways to a depth of at least 200 miles behind enemy lines to determine the enemy's supply routes and to note his troop movements.

C: Artillery Adjustment

This normally consisted of TAC R pilots adjusting the fire of long-range artillery fire (155 mm guns to 8-in. howitzers) in areas where light aircraft such as L-4s or L-5s could not operate safely. These missions could have been either planned with the use of target photographs, or they could be run at any time by a ground station requesting information from a TAC R aircraft about targets in the area in which it operated.

D: Merton Oblique Photo Cover

These missions were normally flown after a specific request from the artillery commander of a given area, and the gridded photographs were used in planning fields of fire for his guns.

E: Photographic Missions

Under certain conditions, for example a 4,000 ft ceiling or a penetration in excess of 150 miles, it was impractical to send the F-5, which was unarmed, to take high-altitude photographs, so TAC R aircraft were used for these missions.

When operating both its TAC R squadrons, the 10th PRG could complete approximately 30 missions a day and a breakdown of a typical day's operations was as follows:

a. 20 Area Searches
b. 4 Route Recces
c. 2 Merton Obliques
d. 4 Artillery Adjustments

Photo Reconnaissance

The Photo Recce squadrons assigned to the 10th PRG used the F-5, which was the camera version of the P-38 Lightning. Unlike the F-6s of the TAC R squadrons, the F-5 was not armed and its pilots flying single-plan missions had to rely on altitude, speed, or evasive action for protection. The F-5s normally ranged 100-150 miles from their bases, but at times, on airfield coverage for example, went as deep as 250-275 miles. The comparative F-4/5 designation to the fighter version is as follows:

F-4 – P-38E	F-4A – P-38F
F-5A/B – P-38G	F-5C – P-38H
F-5E/F – P-38J	F-5E/G – P-38L

The standard F-5 camera installation consisted of two 24-in. cameras, the K-17 or the K-22, with a seven degree side-lap. Most variations of this were simply the substitution of cameras of longer focal length for extreme high-altitude work, or 12-in. or shorter focal length cameras when the ceiling was too low for the 24 in, or a special "dicing" mission was being flown.

For dicing missions, such as those flown over Normandy, the F-5s carried a 12-in. focal length nose camera tilted downward at a 10-degree angle and two 6-in. focal length oblique cameras, one on each side, aimed slightly forward from right angles to the aircraft's line of flight, which gave an uninterrupted coverage of more than 180 degrees (see illustration of camera installation).

To provide the Army with 1:10,000 scale photographs with a camera of 24-in. lens, F-5 pilots normally flew at 24,000 ft, but at times they did operate as high as 35,000 ft using a 40-in. lens. On

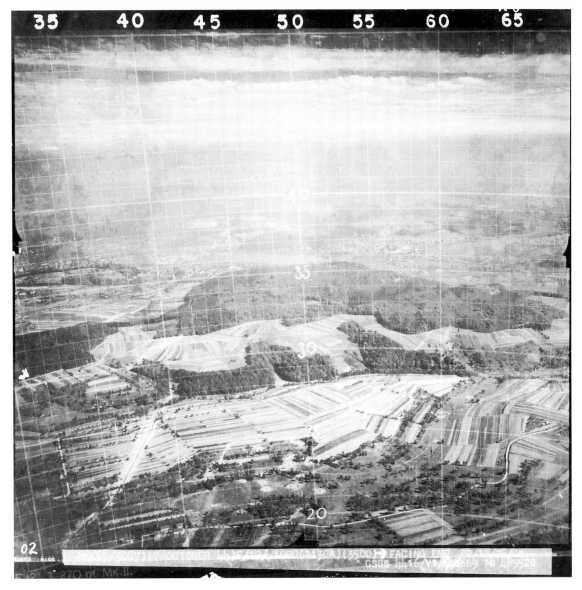

ABOVE: An example of a Merton Gridded Oblique photograph. (*credit: Henry Lewis*)

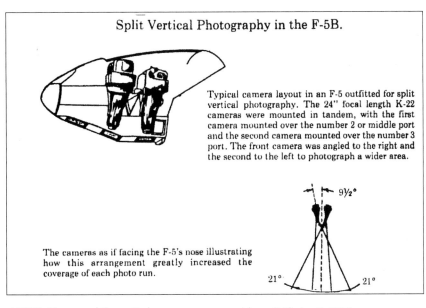

Split Vertical Photography in the F-5B.

Typical camera layout in an F-5 outfitted for split vertical photography. The 24" focal length K-22 cameras were mounted in tandem, with the first camera mounted over the number 2 or middle port and the second camera mounted over the number 3 port. The front camera was angled to the right and the second to the left to photograph a wider area.

The cameras as if facing the F-5's nose illustrating how this arrangement greatly increased the coverage of each photo run.

9½°

21°   21°

ABOVE: Diagram of the vertical camera arrangement in an F-5B. (*credit: USAF*)

RIGHT: A vertical camera installation in an F-5E Lightning. (*credit: Air Force Museum*)

many high priority missions, when weather conditions prohibited high-altitude photography, straight-line courses at 6,000 ft using 6-in. cameras which produced 1:12,000 scale photos were flown. Later, 12-in. cameras were designed that could be operated as low as 5,000 ft. However, these missions were kept to a minimum since light *flak* at this altitude was murderous. When photographs were extremely urgent or low-level close-ups were required, the 10th's F-5 pilots would use the "dicing" technique. For these "dicing" photographs, they would make a high-speed pass over the target area at about 50 ft and depart before any *flak* gunners would normally have time to react.

Photo Reconnaissance missions were generally divided into the following types:

A: Strips and Mosaics
These missions involved the photographing of an entire battle zone and areas of proposed operations, lines of communications, and areas of "no man's" land.

B: Pinpoints
Pinpoint missions involved the photographing of specific targets such as airfields, bridges, marshaling yards, roads, gun positions, command posts, etc.

C: Front-line Coverage
This was the detailed photography of the immediate front line areas to determine the enemy defenses, gun positions, priority targets, etc., and was usually performed on a daily basis.

D: Bomb Damage Assessment
These missions involved photographing targets within a few minutes after they were bombed in order to determine the extent of damage.

Night Photo Reconnaissance
The 155th Night Photo Reconnaissance Squadron used the F-3A, the camera version of the A-20J Havoc, with a crew consisting of a pilot, navigator, and an aerial gunner, and flew single-plane missions involving up to 400 mls of flying. At first the F-3As were armed with twin .50 caliber machine guns in the top turret, but these were later replaced by a tail-warning device which rang a bell in the pilot's cockpit if an enemy approached from the rear. If a "bogey" approached, the F-3A's only defense was violent evasive action. The greatest problem for the night flying F-3As was navigation, and of all the systems tried, the GEE system was the most successful. Because of the problems of navigation, attack from *flak* (both German and Allied) and night fighters, night photo missions were a costly effort in terms of both men and equipment; personnel casualties

exceeded 30 percent and 100 percent of the aircraft used were either damaged or destroyed by the end of the war, but the significance of their work seemed to make the effort worthwhile.

Later in the war, Microwave Early Warning (MEW) was used to check areas for enemy aircraft prior to a mission, and in some incidences the F-3As were escorted by P-61 night fighters; but even with the close co-ordination with Allied anti-aircraft batteries, the dangers of AA fire and navigation were never completely eliminated.

The F-3As were equipped with one of two different types of camera equipment and flew two different types of missions; pinpoint or strip photo runs.

F-3As equipped with the D-2 Flash Unit or Edgerton Lamp as it was more commonly called operated between 2000 and 3000 ft altitude and used a K-19 or K-29 camera with a 12-in. lens. This camera, which could make 180 exposures, was synchronized with a powerful condenser (the Edgerton Lamp) which during the photo run discharged a light intensity of 200,000,000 candle power every three seconds and produced photographs of excellent quality.

F-3As equipped with the M-46 flash-bomb system operated between 6,000-10,000 ft and carried two 12 in cameras. In this system the F-3A carried ten M-46 Flash Bombs, which after being released, were ignited at a given time by a set fuse, and the 800,000,000 candle-power light tripped the camera through a photo-electric cell.

"Dicing" Missions
The extremely low-level missions flown by the 10th Photo Reconnaissance Group over the Normandy beaches in May 1944 and later over the Seine and Moselle River areas became known as "Dicing" missions. The term "Dicing" is a British slang expression for an extremely dangerous or risky mission, i.e., throwing the dice against death. Since these missions involved considerable risk to the pilots involved, the name was appropriately applied.

Over Normandy's beaches the missions were flown at an average altitude of 25 ft, and always during low tide when the broadest area of the beaches could be seen and the maximum number of German obstacles would be exposed to the camera's eye.

The pilots would fly from Chalgrove, England at minimum altitude to their respective zones of the coastline and turn to make the camera run. Usually the beaches were centered with the land to the pilot's left and the Channel to his right, and then the pilot would push his throttle all the way forward and set the cameras at "run-away speed" and head over the beach at approximately 375 mph. With the nose camera and the oblique cameras filming simultaneously with overlapping coverage, a broad coverage of the target area could be obtained in one pass.

LEFT: An artist's impression of Lieutenant Garland A. York's "dicing" run over the Normandy beaches. (*credit: Ben Rosen*)

BELOW: An example of a bomb damage assessment photograph taken along the Normandy coast. (*credit: Edgar A. "Jack" Poe*)

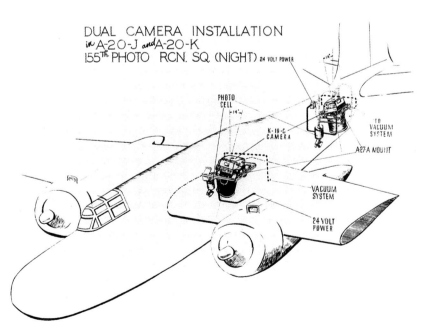

ABOVE: The camera installation of an F-3A Havoc equipped with M-46 flash bombs for illumination. (*credit: Air Force Museum*)

BELOW: The astro dome which replaced the ball turret in F-3As. A tail warning radar was also mounted in the vertical tail surface. (*credit: Air Force Museum*)

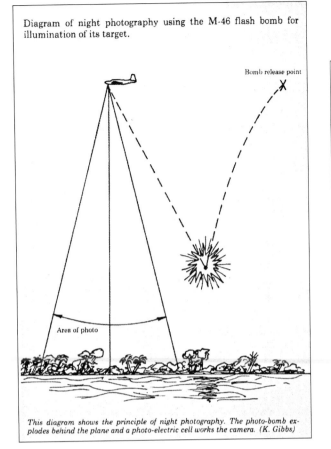

Diagram of night photography using the M-46 flash bomb for illumination of its target.

Bomb release point

Area of photo

This diagram shows the principle of night photography. The photo-bomb explodes behind the plane and a photo-electric cell works the camera. (K. Gibbs)

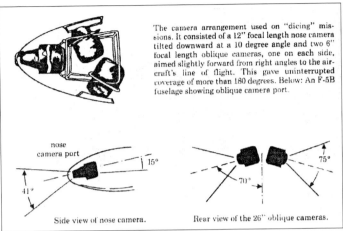

The camera arrangement used on "dicing" missions. It consisted of a 12" focal length nose camera tilted downward at a 10 degree angle and two 6" focal length oblique cameras, one on each side, aimed slightly forward from right angles to the aircraft's line of flight. This gave uninterrupted coverage of more than 180 degrees. Below: An F-5B fuselage showing oblique camera port.

nose camera port

15°

41°

Side view of nose camera.

75°

70°

Rear view of the 26" oblique cameras.

ABOVE: Diagram of "dicing" camera layout in an F-5. (*credit: USAF*)

LEFT: Diagram of night photography. (*credit: K. Gibbs*)

BELOW: An excellent view of the forward-facing and oblique camera ports on a 30th PS F-5A. (*Air Force Museum*)

North American F-6C Mustang, s/n 43-12400, *Mazie, Me and Monk*, Captain E.B. "Blackie" Travis, 12th Tactical Reconnaissance Squadron, 67th Tactical Recon Group, Middle Wallop, England, early Spring 1944. Assigned 10th PRG in mid-June 1944: This Mustang was one of the most famous, if not the most famous, aircraft assigned to the 10th PRG during its tour of combat. *Mazie, Me And Monk* was one of the first four Mustangs assigned to the 12th TRS and the only one of the four to survive the war. She flew the squadron's first Mustang mission with Captain Travis at the controls on 3 January 1944 and was still flying 172 missions later. Her final mission was on 28 May 1945 flown as ZMJA by Lieutenant Robert Worrell (even though the war was over these late May sorties were still recorded as a combat mission). This profile shows the aircraft as it appeared in the Spring of 1944. The aircraft, named after Captain Travis' wife Mazie, himself and crew chief S/Sgt. Jesse "Monk" Davidson, did not go unscathed in its long combat history. It was badly shot up by *flak* on four occasions, transferred twice, declared war-weary, and in spite of all odds, soldiered on as ZMJO, ZMJQ(bar) and finally as ZMJA in the 12th TRS. She was flown during her long tour of combat by virtually every pilot in the 12th TRS, Colonel Russ Berg, and at least two 15th TRS pilots.

North American F-6D Mustang, s/n 44-12812, *Kitten*, Lieutenant Alfred O. Frick, 15th Tactical Reconnaissance Squadron, 10th Photo Reconnaissance Group, Fürth, Germany, May 1945: *Kitten* was assigned to Lieutenant Frick during the latter stages of his second tour of duty with the 15th TRS. She is portrayed as she appeared at Fürth during the last few days of the war. Her crew chief was S/Sgt. Fred Remian.

North American F-6C Mustang, s/n 43-12467, *The Eyes of the World* (left)/*Nankie-Poo* (right), Lts. Jackson Marshall and Fred "Link" Trenner, 15th Tactical Reconnaissance Squadron, 10th Photo Reconnaissance Group, St. Dizier, November 1944: This Mustang is portrayed as it appeared in November 1944. It was one of the Squadron's initial allocation of Mustangs and from what can be seen in the supporting photograph, it had flown a combination of about 60 photo and visual recce missions at this point in time. During its long combat tour, it was flown by a number of pilots, but is most associated with Lieutenant Fred Trenner, who named it *Nanki-Poo*. The end of the trail for 5MJX came in March 1945, when Lieutenant Norbert Kirkpatrick crash-landed her after a rough mission. She continued to serve as a "hangar queen" for spare parts.

North American F-6D Mustang, s/n 44-14775, *Tampa Joe*, Lieutenant M. Leo Elliott, 12th Tactical Reconnaissance Squadron, 10th Photo Reconnaissance Group, Fürth, Germany May 1945: *Tampa Joe* was named after a hometown friend of Lieutenant Leo Elliott, and squadron artist Lloyd Hoobery presented the fact beautifully on this Mustang. Elliott flew this aircraft on the majority of his missions during his tenure with the Squadron. It was apparently used at least once for a dicing mission since a photo taken at Giraumont, France shows it with a drop tank camera attached to its left wing (see profile of F-6D 5MJM.)

North American F-6D Mustang, s/n 44-14715, *Miss Minookie* (right), Captain Dale Goodermote, 15th Tactical Reconnaissance Squadron, 10th Photo Reconnaissance Group, Fürth, Germany, May 1945: This was the second aircraft assigned to Dale Goodermote with the name that recounted the historic lament of lonely servicemen. The first was an F-6C, s/n 42-103620 coded 5MJE, which was salvaged in February 1945.

North American F-6C Mustang, s/n 43-25162, *Hotshot*, Lieutenant Robert "Hotshot" Gardner, 12th Tactical Reconnaissance Squadron, 10th Photo Reconnaissance Group, Fürth, Germany, May 1945: Another of Lloyd Hoobery's masterpieces adorns the nose of Bob Gardner's F-6C *Hotshot*. Gardner obtained his nickname due to his resemblance to "Hotshot Charlie" from the wartime comic strip "Terry and the Pirates" and for his speedy landings. Gardner scored his only victory in this Mustang.

North American F-6C Mustang, s/n 42-103213, '*Azel* (left)/*Boomerang* (right), Lieutenant Stanley Newman, 162nd Tactical Reconnaissance Squadron, 10th Photo Reconnaissance Group, Fürth, Germany, May 1945: *Azel*' displays the red and white checkerboard and red spinner of the newly assigned 162nd TRS. The colors of the name *Boomerang* on the right side of the nose were black with a yellow border. Lieutenant Newman was flying this Mustang when he shot down an Fw 190 over Czechoslovakia on 8 May 1945.

North American F-6D Mustang, s/n 44-14306, *Lil Margaret*, Captain Clyde B. East, 15th Tactical Reconnaissance Squadron, 10th Photo Reconnaissance Group, Fürth, Germany, May 1945: *Lil Margaret* was named after Clyde East's wife and was his favorite aircraft during his two tours of duty with the 15th TRS. It went through a series of marking changes during the period in which Clyde flew it. Initially the aircraft had no name on it, and displayed two large swastikas under the left windscreen. As his victories grew in number, the kill markings were changed to German crosses and the name *Lil Margaret* first appeared in small "hand-written" script above the left exhaust stacks. This profile illustrates the aircraft in its final and most well known markings, with the name in red "Old English" script and the 13 victory marks indicating East's "final" score. In reality, his logbook indicates 14 kills. The additional victory, a Fieseler Storch, was noted in his logbook but never claimed because of the edict of General Weyland. After Captain East departed for the United States at the end of the war, *Lil Margaret* flew on for a while as *Lil Marie* of the 31st PS and was coded 8VJG.

North American F-6D Mustang, s/n 44-14735, *Pride of the Bluegrass*, Lieutenant John "Red" Ellis, 12th Tactical Reconnaissance Squadron, 10th Photo Reconnaissance Group, Fürth, Germany, May 1945: Red Ellis' Mustang indicates his pride in his native state of Kentucky, the "Bluegrass State", and that point is illustrated by another of Lloyd Hoobery's paintings. In his painting, Hoobery has included the name of the aircraft accompanied by a jitterbugging "Kentucky Colonel" decked out in a blue and white "zoot suit." Ellis was assigned this Mustang after his F-6C was destroyed on 5 April 1945 and used it during the remainder of his combat tour. The aircraft was severely damaged in a taxiing accident in October 1945 and salvaged.

North American F-6C Mustang, s/n 43-25174, Millie, *My Baby And Me*, Lieutenant Haylon R. "Joe" Wood, 15th Tactical Reconnaissance Squadron, 10th Photo Reconnaissance Group, Fürth, Germany, May 1945: Lieutenant Wood was assigned this aircraft after his transfer from the 363rd TRG to the 15th TRS and flew the vast majority of his missions in it. He decided on the name after seeing *Mazie, Me And Monk* on the 12th TRS flight line and seized upon the three "M" arrangement as the prototype for *Millie, My Baby And Me*. (The aircraft was named after his wife and child and himself). He was an extremely aggressive and controversial pilot and as noted in Appendix Three, this part of his personality is probably the reason he was never given credit for his 3.5 victories. The noted historian, Dr. Frank Olynyk, has chosen to be more reasonable in his studies and honors Lieutenant Wood's victory claims.

North American F-6D Mustang, s/n 44-14675, Lieutenant Leland A. "Lee" Larson, 15th Tactical Reconnaissance Squadron, 10th Photo Reconnaissance Group, Fürth, Germany, May 1945: This profile illustrates 5MJM as it appeared after Larson obtained "sole ownership" of this Mustang. Originally, he shared it with Lieutenant Henry Lacey, who named it *Nancy*. The name appeared in black "Old English" script under the exhaust stacks on the left side of the nose. At that time it also displayed four German crosses signifying Lieutenant Lacey's victories (it is assumed that, at this time, Lieutenant Lacey was the "senior partner" and his markings took precedence). Once it became solely Lieutenant Larson's aircraft, the name came off and it displayed six German crosses indicating his final score. This profile also shows the aircraft with a wing tank camera mounted on its left wing.

North American F-6C Mustang, s/n 42-103615, *Shovelnose and Handlebar*, Lieutenant Edward Kenny, 12th Tactical Reconnaissance Squadron, 10th Photo Reconnaissance Group, Fürth, Germany June 1945: Lieutenant Kenny was the last of several assigned pilots during this Mustang's service in the squadron. Prior to Lieutenant Kenny, its assigned pilot was Lieutenant Robert Hansen and the only artwork it sported was the Vargas girl under the left windscreen and it remained this way until after war's end. When news that the Bob Hope/Jerry Cologna USO tour was heading for Fürth, Lloyd Hoobery struck again and decorated ZMJE with an excellent caricature of Bob Hope and gave it the name. "Handlebar" was in reference to Jerry Cologna's trademark handlebar moustache. Bob Hope enjoyed the painting and made reference to it in his book *I Never Left Home*.

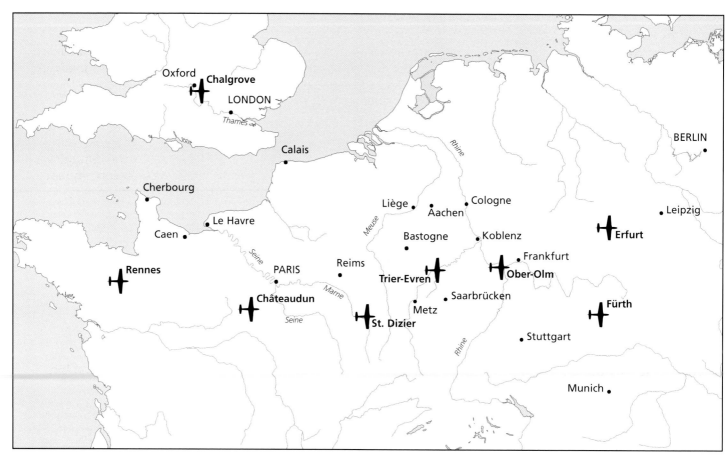

 Airfields of the 10th PRG

APPENDIX SEVEN

CHANGES IN GROUP ORGANIZATION: SEPTEMBER 1941-JUNE 1945

September, 1941
73rd Observation Group
Headquarters activated

November, 1941
HQ, 73rd Observation Group
HQ & HQ Squadron
12th Observation Squadron
16th Observation Squadron
22nd Observation Squadron
91st Observation Squadron

January, 1942
HQ, 73rd Observation Group
HQ & HQ Squadron
16th Observation Squadron
22nd Observation Squadron
91st Observation Squadron

July, 1942
15th Observation Squadron
28th Observation Squadron
91st Observation Squadron

April, 1943
HQ, 73rd Reconnaissance Group
14th Liaison Squadron
15th Recon. Squadron (Fighter)
28th Recon. Squadron (Bomber)
91st Recon. Squadron (Fighter)

August, 1943
HQ, 73rd Tactical Recon. Group
15th Tactical Recon. Squadron
28th Tactical Recon. Squadron
152nd Tactical Recon. Squadron

November, 1943
HQ, 73rd Tactical Recon. Group

December, 1943
73rd Tactical Recon. Group
Redesignated as
HQ, 10th Photo Group (Recon)

February, 1944
HQ, 10th Photo Recon. Group
30th Photo Squadron

March 1944
HQ, 10th Photo Recon. Group
30th Photo Squadron
31st Photo Squadron
34th Photo Squadron

April 1944
HQ, 10th Photo Recon. Group
30th Photo Squadron
31st Photo Squadron
33rd Photo Squadron

Late June 1944
HQ, 10th Photo Recon. Group
31st Photo Squadron
33rd Photo Squadron
34th Photo Squadron
155th Night Photo Squadron
15th Tactical Recon. Squadron
12th Tactical Recon. Squadron
(detached)

August 1944
HQ, 10th Photo Recon. Group
12th Tactical Recon. Squadron
15th Tactical Recon. Squadron
31st Photo Squadron
34th Photo Squadron
155th Night Photo Squadron

October 1944
HQ, 10th Photo Recon. Group
12th Tactical Recon. Squadron
15th Tactical Recon. Squadron
31st Photo Squadron
155th Night Photo Squadron

February 1945
HQ, 10th Photo Recon. Group
12th Tactical Recon. Squadron
15th Tactical Recon. Squadron
31st Photo Squadron

April 1945
HQ, 10th Photo Recon. Group
12th Tactical Recon. Squadron
15th Tactical Recon. Squadron
162nd Tactical Recon. Squadron
31st Photo Squadron

A LAST WORD: THE MEN ON THE GROUND

As with most operational histories, the bulk of this narrative is devoted to the pilots and the missions that they flew. It was the pilots that carried out the 10th Photo Reconnaissance Group's assignments, but they could not have successfully performed the task without the dedicated labor of their ground crews and other support personnel. It took the combined efforts of the aircraft ground crew, the camera and photo lab personnel, refueling teams, and numerous other staff personnel to prepare the pilot and his aircraft for each and every mission. The job for the crews on the ground was even more difficult in the Ninth Air Force since it operated from advance airfields from shortly after D-Day throughout the remainder of the war. A good example of their endurance and dedication was when they had to endure the bitter cold and snows of the winter of 1944-1945 while keeping their assigned aircraft in first-class condition. The following poem written by an unknown author honors all of these unsung heroes who labored so hard to "...keep them flying."

THE FORGOTTEN MAN

Through the history of world aviation
Many names have come to the fore;
Great deeds of the past in our memory will last
As they're joined by more and more.
When man first started his labor
In his quest to conquer the sky
He was the designer, mechanic, and pilot
And he built a machine that would fly.
The pilot was everyone's hero.
He was brave, he was bold, he was grand;
As he stood by his battered old biplane
With his goggles and helmet in his hand.
To be sure, these pilots all earned it,
To fly then you had to have guts.
And they blazed their names into the Hall of Fame
On wings with bailing wire struts
But for each of those flying heroes
There were thousands of little renown
They were the men who worked on the planes
But kept their feet on the ground.
We all know the name of Lindbergh,
And we have read of his flight into fame.
But think, if you can, of his maintenance man,
Can you remember his name?
And think of our wartime heroes,
Gabreski, Jabara, and Scott.
Can you tell me the names of their crew chiefs?
A thousand to one you cannot.
Now, pilots are highly trained people,
And wings are not easily won,
But without the work of the maintenance man
Our pilots would march with a gun.
So when you see the mighty aircraft
As they mark their path through the air
The grease-stained man with a wrench in his hand
Is the man who put them there.

author unknown

INDEX